Anonymity and Death

Anonymity and Death: the Fiction of B. Traven

Donald O. Chankin

The Pennsylvania State University Press
University Park and London

Library of Congress Cataloging in Publication Data

Chankin, Donald O   1934–
    Anonymity and death.

    1. Traven, B. I. Title.
PT3919.T7Z6   813'.5'2   75–1376
ISBN 0–271–01190–4

Designed by Andrew Vargo

Printed in the United States of America

Contents

v

Contents

Preface

B. Traven, the author whose desire for anonymity was so intense that his real name may never be known, is now receiving recognition in spite of himself. Much of Traven's current popularity derives from the movie version of his novel *The Treasure of the Sierra Madre*. Indeed, my interest in Traven began with the discovery that this film was based on a fine novel. I then read *The Death Ship*, a "sea story" comparable to those of Melville and Conrad, and I realized that the nearly unknown author was a major novelist. As interest in Traven began to increase, *Ramparts* magazine published a series of "Conversations with B. Traven" by Judy Stone. The person interviewed in these 1967 articles steadfastly maintained that he was "Hal Croves," Traven's agent. When, like Judy Stone, I found that the facts concerning Traven's birth and childhood were impossible to come by, I decided to use Traven's insistence on his separate identities as a basis for approaching his works, which reveal an intense preoccupation with the problem of identity and the fear of death.

One reason for the lack of recognition accorded Traven in America has been the doubt about his nationality and the consequent omission of his works from anthologies of literature. He reportedly had been a German revolutionary under the name Ret Marut; his books first appeared in Germany; and he died a Mexican citizen.

But he claimed he was born in Chicago, used Americans as protagonists in his best works, and rewrote his books in English for publication in America. Pragmatically, he should be regarded as an American writer. He can then be evaluated in the light of his possible relationship to the hard boiled school of writing, and also to Jack London—another writer of adventure narratives. He can also be evaluated in relation to works involving social protest and in relation to the work of Melville, whose whaling ship is the model for an illicit tramp steamer in *The Death Ship*.

One sign of increasing interest in Traven was the Conference on the Life, Literature and Cinema of B. Traven held at the University of Arizona in April 1974. Among those participating were Señora Rosa Elena Lujan, Traven's widow, and Gabriel Figueroa, Traven's closest friend and also Mexico's leading cinematographer. Señor Figueroa was the director and cameraman for several films made in Mexico from works by Traven, among them the award-winning *Macario*. Further interest was indicated when Hill & Wang recently republished Traven's major works in both hard and soft-cover editions. (*The Death Ship* has been in print as a Collier paperback since 1962.) I hope that my book, intended to be the first full length study in English of Traven's fiction, will contribute toward gaining Traven the critical recognition he deserves in the country he claimed as his own.

It was in Professor Edwin H. Miller's American Literature class at New York University that I first learned the possibilities of applying the insights of psychology to literature. He encouraged me to use the psychoanalytic method in an analysis of Traven's works, and he read and criticized the manuscript in its initial stages. I owe special thanks to Professor Rolf Recknagel of East Germany, whose *B. Traven: Beiträge zur Biografie* contains all the facts that can be determined about B. Traven. He generously offered to share with me all of the information in his files; several of the essays by Traven that I cite in my text I could not have otherwise obtained. Frances Tish read, criticized, and made valuable suggestions in the writing of the manuscript. Professor Heinz K. Henisch of the Pennsylvania State University, who has read nearly everything by and about Traven, offered some valuable advice in the final stages of the book.

1

Traven Torsvan, Hal Croves, and B. Traven: The Man, the Agent, and the Writer

The mystery of B. Traven's identity may never be completely resolved, so successfully did the man hide behind his mask of pseudonyms. But in a will written on 4 March 1969 in Mexico City, three weeks before his death, he asserts for the first time that all of the names associated with him are indeed his. He states that his name is "Traven Torsvan Croves," that he was born in Chicago, Illinois, on 3 May 1890, the son of Burton Torsvan and Dorothy Croves de Torsvan, and that "in his long literary career he has used as noms de plume B. Traven and Hal Croves."[1] His name is given here in the Spanish fashion, with the mother's name "Croves" last. However, there is no birth certificate under "Traven" or "Torsvan" or "Croves" registered with the Cook County Clerk,[2] and it is unlikely at this late date that any documentary proof of Traven's birth or original nationality will be found.

The absence of documentation concerning Traven's birth and early life and his lifelong passion for anonymity contribute to our understanding of the major themes of his work: loss of identity and fear of anonymous death. His protagonists are society's underdogs who, lacking documentary proof of their identity or nationality, are condemned to brutal labor on death ships and in the *monterías* [labor camps] of the Mexican jungle, or to a futile search for gold in the Sierra Madre mountains. Anonymous and un-

1

mourned death stalks his characters on the seas and in the jungle.

Traven's novels first appeared in Germany, beginning with *The Death Ship* in 1926.[3] This book was followed by two other major novels, *The Treasure of the Sierra Madre* (1927), and *The Bridge in the Jungle* (1929). With the manuscript of *The Death Ship* Traven had enclosed a letter stating that although his "life story would not disappoint" his readers, it is "private" and he would like to keep it that way.[4] The only information given about the author upon the book's publication was that he lived in Mexico.

The three major novels were published in the United States in the 1930s and received much critical acclaim,[5] but again nothing about the author was revealed. In 1938 an article in *Publisher's Weekly* explained why no biographical information was available. Traven, after declining Knopf's offer to publish his novels, agreed only on condition that "no blurbs would be printed on the jackets of Traven's books, no publicity about him, his life, or his present whereabouts. . . . It was further agreed that the advertising would be chaste and modest and the copy would consist mainly of the title, the author's name, the price of the work, and perhaps a line of description." The only other information available at the time was that a Knopf editor, Bernard Smith, was working on the manuscripts supplied by Traven.[6] It was not until thirty-two years later that Smith, in an article in the *New York Times Book Review*, told the full story of how he came to edit the manuscripts.[7] In this article he states that part of his responsibility was to "prevent the issuance of any publicity about Traven."[8] Traven instructed him "over and over again . . . that not one word was ever to be uttered by his publishers or his editor as to his whereabouts, his life, his business, or his personal observations. He would supply no biographical information of any kind to anyone." So faithfully did Knopf adhere to these strictures that it was not until 1947, on the movie set of *The Treasure of the Sierra Madre*, that the identity of the man behind the novels was discovered—or at least almost discovered.

Traven Torsvan, Hal Croves, and B. Traven

In 1946 John Huston began writing letters to Traven about the film version of *The Treasure of the Sierra Madre*, which he was directing, and received in reply long letters with suggestions. Huston, fascinated by the suggestions, wrote asking Traven for an interview.[9] At the Hotel Reforma in Mexico City, Huston, after waiting for several days without receiving any word, was handed a calling card inscribed "Hal Croves, Translator, Acapulco." "Croves" was a "tiny, thin man with gray hair . . . dressed in khaki." He brought a letter from "Traven" which explained that he, Traven, would be unable to meet Huston but that "Croves knew Traven's work better than I do." Huston hired "Croves" as a "technical advisor" for $150 a week, but on the location in Mexico "Croves" did not come up with any worthwhile suggestions. When Huston guessed that "Croves" was Traven and a rumor to that effect spread on the set, "Croves" became angry and began to make suggestions even more ludicrous than those he had been making. He even suggested replacing Walter Huston,[10] the director's father, who played Howard, the old prospector, and who was one of the best actors in the film.

"Croves" departed from the set and the letters to Huston resumed; some were from "Croves," others from "Traven," written on different paper and by different typewriters, but they were clearly the work of one man. The *Life* reporter who covered the story showed a verified photograph of Traven to Humphrey Bogart, who played the role of Dobbs, the film's protagonist. When asked if he recognized the photograph he said, "Sure, pal. I'd know him anywhere, I worked with him for ten weeks in Mexico."[11]

After the story appeared in *Life*, "H. Croves" wrote an angry, nearly incoherent letter denying that he was Traven. "Mr. John Huston, by being convinced . . . that I was Traven, and then paying me a lousy $100 a week, only shows publicly in how low an estimation he is holding Traven." Huston responded more soberly: "Personally, I would deplore any definite proof that Croves and Traven are one. Traven has worked very hard at being mysterious . . . in a world where too much is known about too many."[12] How-

3

ever, the definite proof was forthcoming; an aggressive young Mexican reporter, Luis Spota, traced a check with which "Croves" was reputed to have repaid a loan to a bank in Acapulco.

Spota had been told by an editor, "Whoever discovers Traven will be a great reporter."[13] Now he had a definite lead; checking the names of all foreigners who had deposits in banks in Acapulco, he came up with a "Berick Traven Torsvan." Searching further in Mexican immigration files under "Norteamericanos," Spota uncovered a Traven Torsvan, born in Chicago, Illinois, on 5 March 1890. His parents were listed as Burton and Dorothy Torsvan, his occupation engineer. His local residence was found to be in Parque Cachu or Cashew Park, outside Acapulco. Here Spota found a little grey man with bright blue eyes hidden behind dark glasses serving beer and tacos in the shade of cashew trees. He was known locally as "el gringo" and "el mister."[14] While paying several visits to the man and the Mexican woman he lived with, Spota arranged to intercept mail addressed to Cashew Park by bribing a post office employee. Confronted with the evidence of mail addressed to "B. Traven," the little grey man sought to deny his identity with a remarkable series of explanations. "B. Traven" was his cousin; he ("el gringo") was only one of a group of writers published as B. Traven; some of B. Traven's works were written by a woman (Esperanza Lopez Mateos, Traven's first Spanish translator); B. Traven was dead; B. Traven was alive but in a Davos sanitorium in Switzerland. He even offered to write a psychological analysis of B. Traven's personality if he were left alone. At the same time he said, "When I worked in the oil fields, they called me 'The Swede.' That bothered me a great deal and I decided not to use my name 'Torsvan,' typically Scandinavian. From then on I called myself B. Traven."[15]

Obviously a man who can deny and affirm his identity in the same breath is driven by more than a desire to be mysterious. His anguish at being unmasked is apparent in a series of pictures published with Spota's report, which show him in Acapulco trying to avoid being photographed full-face. At Cashew Park he stated, "I

4

am not Mr. B. Traven," and, finally, "Mr. Traven is a solitary man, who hasn't harmed anybody, who does not want honors. He wants only to live in peace." Traven invited Spota back to Cashew Park for dinner. In the center of the table was a roast goose. Traven told a parable in which a hunter was literally sent on a wild goose chase; the story ended with a moral: "He had been sent for a goose, and he found only a phantom, something that did not exist."[16] Spota may not have fully understood the parable, for he published his long article in the magazine *Mañana* which proudly proclaimed the discovery of B. Traven's identity.

Another "interview" with B. Traven was granted in 1966 to another Mexican reporter, Luis Suarez. When the Suarez interview was published, Judy Stone, the art, music, and drama editor of the *San Francisco Chronicle,* was having a series of conversations with "Hal Croves" in his Mexico City home. Stone was surprised to see the Suarez interview described in *Siempre!* as the only one ever granted by the mysterious novelist. But the long story had no photographs of the author, only a full-page shot of the sculptor Frederico Canassi putting the finishing touches to a bust of Traven. The photograph was accompanied by a blurb, "For the first time, the true effigy of the writer is shown to the public." The interview itself was even less revealing, for Traven merely repeated that he was born in Chicago in 1890, and that his real name was Traven Torsvan. Ever since the Spota interview, the rumor had circulated that Traven was somehow connected with Ret Marut, a German actor and radical pamphleteer who had disappeared after the fall of the Bavarian Socialist Republic in 1919. Traven did admit that he had lived in Germany for some time, but affirmed only that "my life belongs to me, my work to the public."[17]

Instead of supplying biographical information, Traven handed Suarez a copy of his "Declaration of Independence from Personal Publicity" for publication in *Siempre!* This document, similar to the one given to his German publisher forty years before, reads:

> I simply do not understand why such a fuss is made about a writer, so that people want to know at what time he gets up, when he break-

fasts, if he drinks, smokes, eats meat, if he plays golf or poker, if he is married or single. My work is important, I am not; I am only a common, ordinary worker. The God of nature granted me the gift of writing books, therefore I am obliged to write books instead of baking bread. In making them, I am no more important than the typographer of my books, than the worker who labors in the factory that makes the paper for my books; I am not more important than the binder of my books or the woman who wraps them or the sweeper of the floors in the office that handles my books. Without their aid and good will there would be no books for the readers, it would do no good that I could write them. Nevertheless, I have never heard of the reader of a good book having asked for the autograph of the typographer, the printer, or the binder.

As a postscript Traven added: "My personal life would not disappoint the readers, but it is my own affair and I want to keep it so."[18] Thus "B. Traven" spoke directly to an interviewer for the first and last time in his life, only to refuse to talk about himself.

In the interviews with Judy Stone, "Croves" refused to admit that he was Traven and spoke about the author only in the third person, as "Torsvan" had done with Spota. (The Suarez interview had been given on the condition that the name "Croves" be omitted from the story, although Suarez did report that Traven's friends called him "Hal.") The Stone interviews present the image of a frail 76-year-old man, nearly deaf and with failing eyesight, stubbornly clinging to his separate identities and talking about himself in the third person. The man had lived so long with his separate identities of B(erick) Traven Torsvan, the American turned Mexican citizen; Hal Croves, the writer's "agent"; and B. Traven, the author, that he was determined to die with them still intact. As soon as Stone met him at his home in Mexico City he cried out: "Forget the man! What does it matter if he is the son of a Hohenzollern prince or anyone else?" Traven was here alluding to the rumor that he was the illegitimate son of Kaiser Wilhelm II, a rumor which he himself may have started.[19]

Although Traven did nothing to elucidate the mystery, he did make interesting comments to Stone about his works. But "Hal

Croves" maintained that it was not easy to understand the books, for sometimes it took many years even for him to understand their full meaning.[20] Occasionally, when "Croves" caught himself slipping into the role of Traven, he would correct himself. He mentioned the time a few years back when his wife nursed him to health after he had been near death. His wife, though, had apparently not saved Traven, but Croves: " 'I'm not talking about Traven,' he said carefully. 'I'm talking about myself.' "[21] The reasons for Traven's role-playing are problematic; his widow, who attempted to clear up the mysteries and to set the record straight, accomplished little in either direction.

Traven's widow, Rosa Elena Lujan, purportedly released information about him shortly after his death on 26 March 1969. Some facts had already been ascertained: he had become a Mexican citizen in 1951, and had married Rosa Elena Lujan, who had been his literary collaborator, in 1957 in San Antonio, Texas.[22] It also seems that he had entered Mexico for the first time at Tampico about 1913, probably after being shanghaied and jumping ship like his fictional counterpart Gales of *The Death Ship*.[23] He entered Mexico for good in 1923, and by 1925 he was in Chiapas province in southernmost Mexico, where he was known to the Indians as "Engineer Torsvan" and "Torsvan the photographer."[24] He was also an amateur archeologist, making some significant discoveries of Mayan ruins.[25] After Spota found him in Acapulco, he divided his time between the jungles of Chiapas and Mexico City, where he later bought a house near the Paseo Reforma, in the midst of the city's Zona Rosa or Pink Zone.[26] Señora Lujan, in her release to the press, repeated the information already stated in Traven's will, that he was born in Chicago on 3 May 1890, of Norwegian-English parentage. She adds that he was in Germany before and after his first trip to Mexico, and that he was in fact the radical editor Ret Marut, who escaped from Germany in the 1920s after being sentenced to death for treason.[27]

The origins of Ret Marut are as obscure as those of "B. Traven." He first appears as a minor actor and director in Germany from

1907 to 1915.[28] When registering as an alien with the police in Dusseldorf in 1912 Marut gave his birthdate as 25 February 1882 and his birthplace as San Francisco. He listed his nationality as English, but when World War I broke out in 1914 his nationality was mysteriously changed to American. To an actress friend he told this fantastic story about his origins: his father was English, his mother Irish; he was born on a ship, his birth papers deposited in San Francisco, and the records destroyed in the 1906 fire and earthquake.[29] In Munich in 1917 Ret Marut began to publish *Der Ziegelbrenner* (*The Brick-Burner*), a radical magazine attacking militarism and nationalism. He was an official in the short-lived Bavarian Socialist Republic in 1919, and when the republic was crushed in the May Day massacre, Marut, about to be tried before a military court that shot most of its prisoners, made his escape.[30]

In April of 1925 the Berlin newspaper *Vorwärts*, the official organ of the Social Democratic Party of Germany, began to serialize a novel called *Die Baumwollplücker* [*The Cotton-Pickers*], by "B. Traven." The address of the author was given as a post office box in Tampico, Tamaulipas, Mexico.[31] Ret Marut's escape to a "far country" had been foreshadowed in a poetic fantasy entitled *Khundar*, which appeared in *Der Ziegelbrenner* in 1920, published while Marut was in hiding. After the collapse of the mythical kingdom described in the work, Khundar says:

> "Salvation will come through questions and searching and wandering! Therefore, let us go wandering where there is truth, wisdom, salvation and light."
> And when he had so spoken, he left from there into a far country that same evening.[32]

Traven never admitted that he was Ret Marut, and there is no hard evidence that they were the same person, only a number of unexplained coincidences. However, everything concerning Traven's life is mysterious; it may be that Traven's secrecy about his identity and his fear and hatred of authority resulted in part from an early—and almost fatal—career as a revolutionary.

Traven's first novel, *The Death Ship*, shows the narrator Gales as a man without a country who, because he has no proof of his American citizenship, is refused a sailor's card by the consuls and other bureaucrats. In this work, and less obviously in others, there is a preoccupation with birth records, official documents, and especially with illegitimacy. Traven may never have been certain of his father's identity, and illegitimacy may lie behind his attempt to hide his identity.

Although problems arise when an author's biography is deduced from his fictional characters, we do know that Gales is an autobiographical character. Traven himself indicated as much in an article,[33] and his widow said that Gales "is the character whom he identified with himself."[34] In *The Death Ship* Gales, in reply to a consul, says: " 'Birth registered?' 'I do not know, sir. When this happened I was too small to remember exactly if it was done or not' . . . . 'Was your mother married to your father?' 'I never asked my mother. I thought it her own business and that it concerns nobody else.' " Later, Gales signs the register of the death ship with an alias: " 'My honest name in the register of a death ship? . . . So I abandoned my good name. I think it was . . . only my mother's name, since it had never been clear if my father had really [added his name] or not. I severed all family connections. I no longer had a name that was by right my own.' "[35] Judy Stone also comes to the conclusion that the "origin of the dilemma about his identity [goes] back to the mystery surrounding his parentage."[36]

Stone even thought it probable that Traven, alias Ret Marut, was the illegitimate son of Kaiser Wilhelm II, although she offers no real evidence to support this theory.[37] In 1967 a German reporter, Gerd Heidemann, published in *Stern* magazine an interview with Rosa Elena Lujan in which she said that her husband believed he was Kaiser Wilhelm's son.[38] Señora Lujan later stated in a letter to Professor Rolf Recknagel that she "never told Heidemann [that Traven] is the son of Wilhelm II although he had asked [her] about it several times." She added, "I know better than anyone else that my husband does not want to speak about his parents."[39]

Traven, like his counterpart Gales, became agitated when the subject of identity was mentioned. Spota quotes Traven as saying, "A person, you, I, can present his birth certificate; but, who can prove that this person is actually the one mentioned in the paper."[40] The problem is posed in a different, calmer, way by Gales to an American consul: " 'It looks, sir, as though you would even doubt the fact that I was born at all?' 'Right, my man. Think it silly or not. I doubt your birth as long as you have no certificate of your birth.' "[41] If the presence of the man does not prove his birth, and the birth certificate does not prove the man's identity, what does confer identity on a man? And how does a sensitive man deal with officials, bureaucrats, consuls, and police when they ask for a non-existent document? He may erect a defense of coined names,[42] and assign one of them to the persona who hides and protects the true self, the author, from the external world.

The coined names, impossible to trace, were designed to protect Traven's anonymity, while at the same time suggesting the Norwegian-English parentage he claimed in his will. "Torsvan" is a more Nordic sounding name than "Traven," but one that may have sounded a little too "typically Scandinavian." Since Traven was probably not legally entitled to use the name of his "Norwegian" father, he fled in panic from the Tampico oil fields when he was called "The Swede."[43] "Croves," a vaguely English-sounding name supposedly his mother's, was to shelter him from the world. Yet when "Croves" was identified with "Traven" by the people on the set of *The Treasure of the Sierra Madre*, he again fled in fear of being discovered or betrayed. Traven probably feared that despite his carefully worked-out system of disguised names, people saw through them to his vulnerable inner self. He was then left with his remaining name, "B. Traven," from which there was no fleeing.

In addition to his names, Traven's two main defenses were his escape to sea and his travels in Mexico. William Weber Johnson reports that Esperanza Lopez Mateos sent him a letter (Johnson thinks the letter may actually have come from Traven) in which the following appears about Traven's early life and education:

One must not forget that he has been a sailor for many years, and that he has had to earn his own living and stand on his own two feet since he was seven. . . . Until he was thirty-five [he] had no more than twenty-six days of education in grammar school. . . . He came to Mexico for the first time when he was twelve, then being cabin boy on a Dutch freighter. He jumped ship on the West Coast of Mexico, stayed for a good time in Mexico, working as an electrician's assistant before returning to his home country. Since then, he has lived in Latin America the greater half of his life, most of the time in Mexico.[44]

The early separation from his mother and the lack of a father or a name that was legally his must have made him feel in danger of losing his identity. He may have imagined himself to be an orphan, rejected by society. Some of this sense of rejection comes through in the following passage in which Gales seems to elaborate on the author's early life:

When I was not yet seven, I was up at four in the morning working for a milkman until six thirty for forty cents a week; from six thirty to nine I worked for a news-agent, who paid me sixty cents a week for running like the devil from residence to residence with an armful of papers; from nine to twelve I shined boots; then there were the afternoon papers; then chopping wood and running to the laundry for ladies; then came the evening papers, and so on until I fell like a stone on the bare floor of a room in Lincoln Avenue, Chic, in which I was allowed to sleep free of charge for washing dishes at night. . . . Before I was ten I shipped as a kitchen-boy on a Spanish tramp, making all the pacific ports from Mexico down to Chile, after having a hurried career as a dumb boy in a circus assisting a clown who couldn't be funny without pushing and fighting a half-starved boy.[45]

Traven's fascination with the sea was probably a result of his sense of being orphaned. His life as a sailor was an attempt to answer the question asked by Melville in *Moby-Dick*: "Where is the foundling's father hidden?"[46] What Newton Arvin said of Melville might be said with more force of Traven: "Imaginatively speaking, psychologically speaking . . . [he] identified himself with the by-blow and the orphan."[47] Traven and Melville were both fatherless at the time of their great voyages and both may have sought a father substitute in the all-male society of the ship. In *The Death*

11

Ship, the ship is where Gales can find a substitute identity and compensation for his uncertain sense of self. The book concludes with a fantasy of omnipotence in which he, a shanghaied stoker, becomes captain of the wrecked death ship. Yet Gales, like Ishmael, is still an orphan in the end.

To compensate further, Traven needed what may be called a fantasy of anonymity. Traven used his travels in Mexico to preserve his anonymity, while at the same time continuing to search for the answer to his precarious sense of identity. The fantasy of anonymity produced *The Treasure of the Sierra Madre* and the Jungle Novels, in which the Mexican Indians rebel to regain their right to live and die without records or documents. The man of illegitimate birth, an outcast from America and Europe, may have been attracted first to the sea, then to Mexico, because he, like one of his characters in *The Death Ship,* read "a couple of hundred stories in imitation of Cooper's *Last of the Mohicans* . . . and another couple of hundred sea-stories and pirate-yarns [that] ambushed his spirit."[48] The life of Natty Bumppo may have inspired Traven's Mexican novels. An orphan reared by Moravian missionaries, Natty finds his true identity by living among the Indians; his changing names, from Leatherstocking and Deerslayer to Hawkeye and La Longue Carabine, reflect the awe and esteem in which they hold him. Only in Mexico, where the Indians were still living in their traditional way, relatively free of Western influence, could Traven find his own frontier. The Indians of Chiapas, having no need for proof of their own identity, would not question the identity of "Señor Torsvan," engineer and photographer; they would accept him as long as they found him simpatico.

In Mexico, Traven was able to act out his fantasy of "being anonymous, or incognito, or a stranger in a strange land," in R. D. Laing's terms. Laing describes cases of the "divided self" and considers them existentially, as manifesting "ontological insecurity."[49] Without a strong sense of identity, Traven may have felt that his true self (Traven, the creative self who was once betrayed) was distinguished from the embodied self that functioned in the external world ("Engineer Torsvan," "Croves, agent and translator"). Feeling more vulnerable and isolated than others, Traven used the defense of anonymity to shield himself from an ever-threatening reality. He probably felt that if he could periodically remove himself from civilization he could start afresh. But it required an incredible expenditure of energy to avoid being discovered. All of Mexico became enemy territory in which he felt almost like a spy, constantly on the lookout for others who might trap him into giving himself away. The demands of money and family led back to civilization, to the oil fields of Tampico, to Cashew Park in Acapulco, and to the film set of *The Treasure of the Sierra Madre*, where he nearly lost his hard-earned anonymity.

When "Croves," afraid of being unmasked as Traven, fled the film set, John Huston theorized: "Traven is a proud man who has retired from active participation in human affairs. In contact with people he disintegrates and becomes ridiculous. Knowing this, his desire to keep the name of Traven free from scorn leads him to disguise himself as somebody else."[50] The small man in baggy khaki trousers was perhaps deliberately making himself appear clownlike to the people who he probably felt were out to discover his true identity. Traven displayed the same ambivalent behavior when he was interviewed: by granting interviews, he called attention to B. Traven, yet asserted "Traven's" right to privacy and spoke about himself in the third person. He thereby focused more attention on himself than his works alone might have. The legend of his royal origin was yet another way of both calling attention to himself and of hiding the real self. All of his defenses and mystifications may be seen as disguised hostility and attempts at protection from those he considered enemies.

Traven, then, was a divided person who sought to protect the inner self from disintegrating when it came in contact with reality. Thus Traven developed his triple identity. Traven Torsvan, the person who insisted that he had a legal name and a rightful identity, existed only on official Mexican immigration and naturalization forms, and appeared only on expeditions to the south of

Mexico, where the Indians, who themselves lacked birth or marriage forms, were unlikely to ask for proof of his identity. Hal Croves was the legal fiction, the agent who assured that B. Traven the writer would never have to speak directly to the outside world. In the Stone interview, Traven says that "HC is the juridical person BT accepted." But so deep was the split between the embodied self who married and lived in Mexico and had a wide circle of friends, and the mysterious self who wrote books, that the former insisted he had no right to be called Traven: "Personally I cannot accept to be called Mr. Traven. I have no right to accept that name. Croves is Croves and Traven is Traven." "Croves's" anguish seems genuine in this interview conducted twenty years after the filming of *The Treasure of the Sierra Madre:* "Why did I ever get mixed up with Traven? I didn't go looking for him. It came to me. Up to the time of the motion pictures, nobody cared about Hal Croves."[51] The memory of the time when the identity of Croves and B. Traven was nearly betrayed is still strong.

The dread of losing identity pervades Traven's works. His best books, *The Death Ship* and *The Treasure of the Sierra Madre,* gain power from the feeling of anxiety provoked in the reader, an anxiety arising from fear of betrayal, leading to loss of identity and disintegration of self. In *The Treasure of the Sierra Madre,* this fear is aroused by betraying one's comrades under the influence of greed. Later works show the author, either as Gales in *The Bridge in the Jungle,* or as the ironic narrator of the Indians' rebellion against oppression in the Jungle Novels, still concerned with the problems of anonymity and identity. In all of the works, the protagonists descend into an underworld-tomb, variously represented by the hold of a death ship, the bowels of the Sierra Madre mountains, a jungle river, and an Aztec tomb. They seek to emerge with a surrogate identity to compensate for society's denial of their birthright. This motif of descent and rebirth is modified in several of the short stories in which Gales plays the role of doctor-medicine man. Gales, by acting as a doctor to the Indians, seeks to gain some control over his fear of anonymous death, a fear that has pursued him from the death ships of America and Europe to the jungles of Mexico. In the final appearance of the theme in Traven's last major work, "Macario," the protagonist becomes a doctor in partnership with his "compadre" or surrogate father, Death. Through the fantasy of his fiction, Traven at last resolves the problem of his paternity.

The actual solution to the mystery of Traven's paternity and identity will probably never be found; in his life his pretense of authorial anonymity seems to have provided him with an adequate defense against disintegration. Freed from the threat of betrayal, he could pursue his vicarious solution to the mystery of his identity in his fiction. B. Traven, he claimed, speaks only in his works. The investigator of the mystery of the man is left with the words of Señora Lujan, his widow, and Gerard Gales, his narrator. Señora Lujan said of her deceased husband: "His official name was B. Traven Torsvan; his real name remains a mystery."[52] Gerard Gales, signing aboard the death ship *Yorikke* with an alias, seems to speak for the author when he says: "I wrote with clear letters that will last until the trumpets of the Last Day are calling, and somebody then will be confused as to how to call me."[53]

2

The Death Ship, The Story of an American Sailor: An Escape Fantasy

The Death Ship (1926) depicts a voyage which takes the protagonist, Gerard Gales, away from civilization and leaves him on a raft in the middle of the ocean. He is alienated from a society which first denies him an identity because he has neither job nor papers, and then threatens to destroy him by condemning him to work on an illicit tramp steamer. The climactic wreck of this death ship represents the severing of the protagonist's last bonds with society and, ironically, with reality. Alone on a raft in a mounting storm, the sole survivor of the shipwreck, Gales, has hallucinations of a haven for his drowned comrade. Thus the basic theme of Traven's works appears: a romantic journey of escape from corrupt, modern industrial civilization, and, paradoxically, the disintegration of the ego in the absence of civilization.

The three books that comprise the novel deal with the shore civilization, the death ship itself, and the escape. Beginning as a "kind of humorous satire on government bureaucracy and the absurdity of passports, it rises into powerful sea fantasia and ends as a *Moby-Dick* of the stokehold."[1] Perhaps the first book is a wild comedy rather than a "humorous satire." It deals with the adventures of Gales, who is stranded in Antwerp without documents or money by the premature departure of his ship, the *Tuscaloosa*. Smuggled across the Dutch border at night by Belgian police, he is arrested in Rotterdam by the Dutch police, who attempt to send him back to Belgium. He goes back to Rotterdam, where the American consul refuses to issue him a new seaman's card without a passport, which in turn cannot be issued without proof of citizenship. "Any bum might step in here and ask me to provide him with legal papers. No, sir"[2] is the consul's answer. Gales stows away on a ship to Boulogne, is promptly arrested by the French police for traveling on a train without a ticket, serves a two-week sentence, is again arrested for "cheating the National railways," and is sentenced to another brief prison term. With many of their citizens unemployed, the nations of post-World War I Europe have no room for foreign nationals who have no means of support. But because Gales has no proof of nationality, he cannot be deported to his native America. Unable to get a berth without his seaman's card, he has become a man without a country: "Y'see, sir. I had no proof of any sort as to my legal existence" (p. 19). Once a man, especially a common deck-hand, steps out of bounds, he is caught in a maze from which there is no escape.

Gales uses humor against the bureaucracy which is denying his existence. The nightmarish situation may recall Kafka, but the treatment is wildly comic, suggesting the silent film comedians, particularly Chaplin as the "little tramp." Gales is the little man at whom the policeman pokes his thumb, evicting him from hotel room, park bench, and train compartment. His involuntary hobo's tour of Europe, with its constant and purposeless movement, recalls Chaplin's journeys. Both men confront a world of mechanism and bureaucracy with stoicism and small gestures of defiance. Gales, like the Tramp, gets short shift from the bureaucrats:

"You are American?"
"Yesser."
"Where is your sailor's identification card?"
"I have lost it, sir."
"Passport?"
"Nosser."
"Citizenship papers?"
"Never had any. Born in the country. Native state—"
"Never mind. Well, what do you want here?" (P. 26)

The second American consul is a carbon copy of the first; police magistrates ask identical questions. Gales develops a routine that he rattles off in reply:

> "And I have no passport either. Nor have I an identification card of the French authorities. No immigration stamp. No customs-house seal. I have no papers at all. Never in all my life did I ever have any papers." (P. 44)

Caught in a lie, he retorts in a way that recalls the shrug of Chaplin's tramp:

> "A rather mysterious ship, your *George Washington*. As far as I know, the *George Washington* has never yet come to Rotterdam."
> "That's not my fault, officer. I am not responsible for the ship." (P. 37)

The underdog has his small triumph when he compels society to admit to its own absurdity:

> "It looks, sir, as though you would even doubt the fact that I was born at all?"
> "Right, my man. Think it silly or not. I doubt your birth as long as you have no certificate of your birth. The fact that you are sitting in front of me is no proof of your birth. Officially it is no proof." (Pp. 55–56)

Society may deny his very existence, but the little man endures by knowing who he is:

> "You ought to have some papers to show who you are," the police officer advised me.
> "I do not need any paper; I know who I am," I said. (P. 48)

But the impasse remains: with neither documentary proof of identity nor a job, Gales's sense of identity as American or sailor does not suffice. The indispensable recognition of identity by society is lacking, and Gales, beneath his comic exuberance, feels the lack. He has lost "the ship that was his home, his very existence, his evidence that he had a place in this world to fill" (p. 13). The premature sailing of the ship is merely the accidental circumstance that creates the crisis in which he is forced to account for himself. The

18

actual source of his alienation is revealed in his conversation with the second American consul:

"Naturalized?"

"No, sir. Native born!"

"Birth registered?"

"I do not know, sir. When this happened, I was too small to remember exactly if it was done or not."

"Then your birth has not been registered."

"I said I do not know, sir."

"But I do know."

"Well, sir, if you know everything beforehand, why do you ask me?"

"Now, don't you get excited here. No reason for that. Was your mother married to your father?"

"I never asked my mother. I thought it her own business, and that it concerns nobody else."

"Right. Excuse me. I was only thinking that the marriage license might be found somewhere." (P. 53)

The ultimate cause of his predicament, then, is his illegitimacy. Behind the aggressiveness of Gales's retorts and possibly behind all his humor lies uneasiness and shame at having his illegitimacy revealed. Only one other mention of his illegitimacy appears in the novel, at the crucial moment when Gales signs aboard the death ship with a pseudonym: "So I abandoned my good name. I think it was anyway only my mother's name, since it had never been clear if my father had really added his name or not. I severed all family connections. I no longer had a name that was by right my own" (p. 113). It is his illegitimacy, rather than the mere accident of the ship's departure, that leads him through the bureaucratic maze to the death ship. The satire on bureaucracy may now be seen as an illegitimate child's projection of his father's failings onto society. His father had abandoned his mother; society, through its bureaucrats, abandons Gales. His father failed to give him a name; society refuses to recognize the identity that was not in fact legally his. The bureaucrats themselves may be seen as father figures repeating the betrayal of Gales's father. The wild comedy and exaggeration with which he

19

tells his story, as well as his aggressive humor and counter-gibes, are defenses to disguise his shame and guilt. And his flight from society to the death ship serves both to hide his shame and to punish himself for his illegitimacy.

He realizes that his flight is from the incessant questions: "Why are you here? Where do you come from? What's your name?" (p. 63). Answering would involve producing proof; not answering would involve an agonizing uncertainty:

> Now, of course, I might just ignore their questions and say nothing. Yet who is he that could stand a hundred questions and answer none? An unanswered question flutters about you for the rest of your life. It does not let you sleep; it does not let you think. You feel that the equilibrium of the universe is at stake if you leave a question pending. A question without an answer is something so incomplete that you simply cannot bear it. You can get crazy thinking of the problems of an unbalanced solar system. The word "Why?" with a question mark behind it is the cause, I am quite certain, of all culture, civilization, progress, and science. (P. 62)

Behind the hyperbole of "an unbalanced solar system" lies anxiety over the knowledge that the name "Gales" was never really his. Thus he begins to still the "flutter" of an unanswered question with a series of lies. He tells the French police that he is a German, and, perhaps predictably, the police and ordinary citizens treat him better than they would have treated an American.

When he signs on the death ship with a pseudonym, the event is described in apocalyptic imagery: "I wrote with clear letters that will last until the trumpets of the Last Day are calling, and somebody then will be confused as to how to call me. 'Helmond Rigby, Alexandria, Egypt'" (p. 118). No reason is given for this particular name, though "Egyptian" possibly evokes "gypsy," which accurately describes both Gales's present condition and that of the ship, a "gypsy of the sea" (p. 250). The Scandinavian-English "Helmond Rigby" recalls "Traven Torsvan Croves," in which the English name is also the surname. Through his narrator, Traven may be asserting his right to the English name "Croves," which he claimed was his mother's and used in his will. Just as the name "Hal Croves" protected Traven from the external world and confused people as to what to call him, so "Helmond Rigby" has the same function for Gales. Pseudonyms protect Gales and Traven from further betrayal.

Traven, who indicated that *The Death Ship* is autobiographical,[3] and who was himself a stoker on a death ship,[4] is writing a disguised version of his own withdrawal from America and Europe. The author's feelings of betrayal are expressed in Gales's final pseudonym of "Pippip," which he assumes for his role as a coaldrag in the death ship's stokehold. Gales-Traven has been made to feel small and insignificant. He resembles Melville's Pip, the castaway, rather than Ishmael, who proudly asserts the name he chooses for the great voyage. Like Ishmael, he is an illegitimate outcast of society. But Gales's journey is one of escape on a tramp steamer, a diminutive voyage whose size is reflected in the name "Pippip." Yet "Pippip," with its phallic connotations, may in itself be an assertion of pride, as Gales's determination to survive the death ship will prove. Traven may also be suggesting Dickens's Pip, who, like Gales, is symbolically linked to an outlaw benefactor. Gales's benefactor is the outlawed ship that seems to be trying to hide her true name. "On her hull was her name: *Yorikke.* The letters were so thin and so washed-off that I got the impression that she was ashamed to let anybody know her true name" (p. 85).

Gales's ostensible reason for leaving "sunny Spain" and boarding the death ship, the belief that a sailor without a berth must take the first job offered to him, is obviously inadequate. The real reason is that he sees the ship as a reflection of himself. "According to international agreements, the name of her home port would have been painted there clearly. Apparently she did not want to betray her birthplace. So you're like me, I thought, without a proper birth-certificate. Bedfellows, hey?" (p. 85). Ship and sailor are illegitimate castaways; the ship, engaged in smuggling arms, has a crew of men without countries who are exploited mercilessly. When it becomes unprofitable to run the ship any longer, the owners will order it sunk for the insurance money. The ship reflects her out-cast crew: the "hull looked pock-scarred . . . [Gales] could not re-member ever having seen anything in the world, ship or no ship, that looked so dreadful and hopeless, and so utterly lost, as did the *Yorikke*" (p. 90).

On the death ship Gales's nightmare is no longer relieved by wild comedy and jest. He struggles to survive hard labor in the ship's antiquated boilers. He begins a grim meditation occasioned by the death's head of the *Yorikke*. Like Hamlet confronting Yorick's skull, Gales must reject his former self and take on the new identity of "Pippip" for his unfamiliar role of coal-drag.[5] Gales's descent into the death ship's stokehold is a turning point in his life, for he is now to be initiated as one of the "living dead": "I, like the rest, was now clothed in striped garments . . . in death sheets, in which I could no longer escape . . . I had become part of the *Yorikke*. Where she was, I had to be; where she went, I had to go. There was no longer any escape to the living" (p. 164). Society's castoff men have been condemned to a lingering existence on a vast floating tomb.

Gales finds himself in a Dantean inferno, whose motto is, "He who enters here will no longer have existence!" (p. 94). Tormented by memories of their former lives and by the knowledge that they can never return to them, the men of the death ship have "vanished from the living" (p. 118). The "inscription over the crew's quar-ters" that forms the epigraph to the second book reads, in part:

> He
> Who enters here
> Will no longer have existence;
> His name and soul have vanished
> And are gone for ever.
> Of him there is not left a breath
> In all the vast world.
> He can never return . . . (P. 95)

Dante's characters are tortured for the evil deeds they committed on earth, but Traven's outcasts are innocent victims. As members of the "black gang," Gales and his fellow stoker, Stanislav, must create their own hell by feeding the nine fires of the *Yorikke*'s furnaces. They are in the inner ring of Traven's inferno, the ninth circle reserved not for traitors to their countries, but for men who have been betrayed by their countries.

Stanislav, for example, is a German born in territory that became part of Poland after World War I. Because he did not choose citizenship in either country within the time allowed by the League of Nations, he is denied passport or seaman's card by both countries. He and the others comprise a foreign legion of the sea. They are either victims of betrayal by their fatherland, as is Stanislav, or by their actual father, as is Gales. The name Stanislav may be an allusion to Razumov of Conrad's *Under Western Eyes*. Conrad, a displaced Pole, uses a Russian protagonist to develop one of his central themes, betrayal and atonement. Traven, the displaced American with a shadowy German past, uses the Polish-German Stanislav to condemn society for betraying men by depriving them of their nationalities. But Razumov is himself guilty of betraying a comrade; Stanislav becomes Gales's only friend and initiates him into the life of the stokehold.

To survive this Inferno Gales must completely "abandon his former existence" by concentrating on his labor: "The whole universe, all religions, all creeds, and my entire consciousness became concentrated in this idea: eleven to six. I had vanished from existence" (p. 165). His most difficult task is helping the firemen replace the fallen grate-bars while they are red-hot and the furnaces are white-hot. Success brings a curious feeling of renewal: "I may justly say, though, that since that night, my first night with grate-bars in the ash-pit, I feel myself standing above the gods. I am free. Unbound. I may do now whatever I wish. I may curse the gods. They cannot punish me any more. No human law, no divine commandments, can any longer influence my doings, because no longer can I be damned. Hell is now paradise" (p. 153). Having descended into the Inferno, he has been initiated before the fires, and has been reborn as a Promethean hero, "Unbound." Now he is beyond punishment by the gods, the bureaucrats, the governmental authorities: beyond punishment by father-figures. Therefore "rebirth had taken place" (p. 166). But this is a rebirth as "Pippip," with no greater expectations than to escape from the doomed ship before it sinks.

With the disguise of his new name he joins a substitute society: "Yet we had proof that people can live without laws and do well. The fire gang had built up among themselves rules which were never mentioned, but, nevertheless, kept religiously" (p. 167). Since he had told the fireman that his "mother was a Parsee" (p. 145), the word "religiously" suggests members of a fire-worshipping sect.

The lowest members of the crew, the fire gang, must provide the power for the journey by religiously feeding the boilers. Their work is rewarded not with sanitary conditions or edible food, but with their own sense of accomplishment. As Stanislav expresses it: "You see, to throw into the tunnel, down to the stoke-hold, some six hundred shovels of coal and do it fine even in heavy weather . . . so that the fire'm stares at you in admiration. . . . You feel so healthy and so sane that . . . the skipper can't feel any better after having brought the ship home through a nasty sea" (pp. 207–8). Although they are the lowest in the ship's hierarchy, their roles have bestowed identities on them and provided a sense of belonging.

Yet their sense of belonging develops within the framework of a continuing journey away from the larger society, and the price they pay for it is fear. The surrogate society keeps the crew in line by threat of punishment—scalding, maiming, or death—if they fail to perform their tasks properly. The ultimate reward is death by drowning at an uncertain date: "the death ticket is all written up; [the owners] have only to fill in the exact date" (p. 171). But the death ship is the only home the men have, and the suspension between life and death becomes their reality. Thus when Gales and Stanislav see a clean new ship, the *Empress*, that is destined to be sunk on her next voyage since faulty engines make her unprofitable, they express their strange love for the *Yorikke*: "Compared to that gilded *Empress*, the *Yorikke* was an honorable old lady with lavender sachets in her drawers. *Yorikke* did not pretend to anything she was not. She lived up to her looks. Honest to her lowest ribs and to the leaks in her bilge" (p. 250). And "I love you, my gypsy of the sea!" (p. 250). Gales is in love with the battered tramp steamer whose body provides a refuge for the tramps within her. For Gales it is a refuge that allows him to hide his shame and guilt; the fear that pervades the voyage substitutes for the anxiety that characterized his journey on land. There, the anxiety below the comic surface was his reaction to the threat of being deprived of his identity. Here the anxiety is translated into a fear of external forces.

The *Yorikke*, then, is the womb that shelters Gales and the entire crew. Since Gales's descent into its stokehold results in his rebirth with a new sense of identity, the ship represents the mother. The flight from society, with its punishing, censorious bureaucrats is a flight from the threatening father. Gales-Traven, the illegitimate orphan, flees society when it demands to know the answer to the secret of his paternity. On the *Yorikke*, the new feeling of belonging serves as a substitute for the father, and the question of paternity need not be considered.

The grotesque journey ends abruptly when Gales and Stanislav are shanghaied to serve as stokers aboard the *Empress*. From a nightmare of living death on the *Yorikke* the men are transported into a dreamlike state as rulers of the wrecked *Empress*. Only the two stokers survive when the ship, scuttled off the West coast of Africa, stands "like a strange tower firmly squeezed in between two rocks" (p. 268). The ship is a "strange tower" because it is inverted: the cabin is downward, and the two laborers of the stokehold have taken over. It stands "firmly" as an erect phallus, representing the power of the formerly impotent stokers. With this symbol Gales-Traven makes a semi-comic gesture of defiance of all authority and all father figures. Little Pippip asserts himself at last. He and Stanislav are "half-partners of one of the latest issues of His Majesty's merchant marine" (p. 273); they are now captains and kings of this "latest issue" which Gales-Traven himself has fathered

25

in his fantasy. They are free at last: no one asks them for "birth-certificate, vaccination certificate, certificate of baptism, certificate of confirmation, marriage license" (p. 271), and they are no longer required to work at stoking furnaces.

Free of society and responsibility, Gales and Stanislav clamber around the ship, exploring the storerooms like children, eating and drinking "caviar and Chablis, or a good English smoked herring washed down with two quarts of stout" (p. 271). They engage in drunken philosophic discourses, pondering whether or not they should be grateful to Destiny. Even their sense of time is destroyed by their absolute freedom: "there now began a banquet which could not have been any better for the original owners of the *Empress* when it was newly born out of the shipyard. I think we got mighty soused. Whether we spent at this banquet one day or four I could never figure out. We got sober and drunk, and sober and drunk again. How many times this happened neither of us could tell" (p. 274). In this parody of a celebration of birth, the men celebrate the rebirth of the *Empress*. They, too, have been "reborn"; they are free to indulge themselves like infants in a nursery. Now that their wish to be free of bureaucracy and the death ship is fulfilled, their only concern is for immediate gratification of the primitive impulses of eating, drinking, and sleeping. Although their predicament is nearly hopeless, the possibility of escape might exist if they were capable of planning it.

The Death Ship shows Gales's continuous retreat from society. He escapes from the shore society of the first book as a member of the crew of the *Yorikke* and the "black gang" of the stokehold. Gales achieves semi-solitude with Stanislav on the *Empress* but he must become completely isolated from men to be fully reborn as Pippip, the orphaned castaway.

Traven, who himself went to sea in a tramp steamer is telling the story of his own withdrawal from society, or at least from America and Europe. Judy Stone says that *The Death Ship* is a "fictionalized account of Traven's own escape from Germany."[6] Then Stanislav would be Gales's double, representing Traven's

26

German experiences and his relationship to the elusive Ret Marut. But the connection is disguised, for Gales "never betrayed to anybody on the *Yorikke* [Stanislav's] true name, . . . together with his story" (p. 187). The climactic episode on the *Empress* can be seen as a dreamlike interlude in which Gales is alone with his past, which he never revealed to anybody.

The interlude is brief; the stokers' wish-fulfilling dream of being in command is shattered when a storm sinks the *Empress*. They escape on a makeshift raft, but, suffering from exposure and thirst, they begin to hallucinate. Stanislav "sees" the *Yorikke* first and then Gales, too, hallucinates: "Now I saw, he was right. Yes, no doubt, there was the *Yorikke*. Floating above the waters in a sort of majestic silence. . . . I could see her quite clearly" (p. 285). The men have projected an image of the tramp ship in which it seems more of a refuge than ever. Stanislav manages to loosen the bonds tying him to the raft, but Gales, entangled in the rope, sees the vision disappear: "I grabbed the cord with all my strength, because I looked around and saw that the *Yorikke* had gone far away. I saw only the sea" (p. 286). Raft and cord are the last remnants of society and ego. Stanislav, who leaves the raft and sheds his last ties to society, dies swimming toward the phantom image of the ship. He has lost all semblance of control over his actions. Only the American, by chance entangled in the remaining bonds, survives to tell the story. The rope, like Melville's monkey rope, is an umbilical cord. Gales has completed his rebirth as a castaway, but he is still tied to society by this slender thread. Complete separation would mean, as it meant to Stanislav, yielding to one's inner fantasies and to death. But the cord tying him to Stanislav, as much his "dear comrade and twin-brother"[7] as Queequegg is Ishmael's, has been cut.

The novel has become a pure fantasy in this last book of dreamlike wrecks and hallucinations. The only alternative to the mazes of bureaucracy and the tortures of the death ship is regression to an infantile state. Gales's final vision suggests that only in death is escape possible. In a hallucination prompted by weariness, Gales imagines that the drowned Stanislav has signed on for a long voyage without papers:

> Yet he did not come up. The Great Skipper had signed him on. He had taken him without papers.
>
> And the Great Skipper said to him: "Come, Stanislav Koslovski, give me your hand. Shake. Come up, sailor! I shall sign you on for a fine ship. For an honest and decent ship. The finest we have. Never mind the papers. You will not need any here. You are on an honest ship. Go to your quarters, Stanislav. Can you read what is written above the quarters, Stanislav?"
>
> And Stanislav said: "Aye, aye, sir. He who enters here will be for ever free of pain!" (P. 287)

The Death Ship ends with this glimpse of a sailor's Paradise that balances the infernal image of the death ships. But rest has come only for Stanislav who, in death, is reunited with the Great Skipper, or father. Gales-Traven must continue to search for the answer to his paternity. As the names "Gales" and "Pippip" imply, he is destined to survive the stormy seas only to remain an orphan.

In an article written at the time of the novel's publication, Traven recognizes that his novel is a "fantasy" in the limited sense that it lacks a "conclusive ending." He says that he could not have written any other ending for "what kept the narrator from perishing . . . has no more to do with *The Death Ship*. (The one who narrates the story must certainly live.) The next line would be the beginning of a new story."[8] Traven disregards the larger implications of the word fantasy and instead stresses, as in the interview with Judy Stone forty years later, that the novel is a satire on bureaucracy. Only the first part can be so classified, but the entire book may be viewed as a fantasy of betrayal and flight. One mischance, the premature departure of the ship on which he was previously signed, coupled with the original act of betrayal by the father, exposes a seemingly civilized world as an irrational maze and turns a civilized Western man into an illegitimate castaway with no hope of a permanent haven. Gales-Traven is, like Ishmael-Melville, an orphan betrayed by a society that denies him paternity and a name. The alternative to living in that society is a sea voyage on which, by hard, dangerous labor, he can combat his death wish and his aggressive impulses against society. But these impulses reappear in the final fantasy in which civilization and its death ships are destroyed.

On the level of social criticism the death ship itself, rather than the shore bureaucracy, is the central symbol. It stands as a powerful, radical symbol of the betrayal and exploitation of anonymous workers, as well as representing a cross section of society. Mark Van Doren, in a perceptive review of the novel, analyzes the ship as a microcosm:

> The narrator . . . finds himself in a little universe whose features sharply resemble the features of the only universe he has ever known. Its rulers—the skipper and the engineers—are staring statues of wood, concrete, and stone, and its populace is a huddle of sickly beasts, deprived long since of pride, wit, feeling, hope. It is not merely that these underdogs are treated cruelly; it is that they are not treated as human beings at all. For the world as our author sees it is not organized on human principles; it is a world of gold and silver and coal, a world of legal papers, of senseless machineries, and of solemn impersonalities.[9]

Beneath the facade of civilization maintained by the shore society stands the corrupt and filthy structure represented by the death ships. Workers, deprived of their identities, are then physically brutalized.

> "Where is the mattress for my bunk?"
> "Not supplied here. Must have your own."
> "Pillows?"
> "Not supplied."
> "What is supplied here, then?" I finally asked.
> "Work," a man answered calmly. (P. 100)

Traven's savage indictment of society is expressed in the metaphor of "modern gladiators . . . greeting . . . great Caesar, Caesar Augustus Capitalismus" (p. 119). After the last profit has been squeezed out of the ship, the men will die for the insurance money:

"We, the gladiators of today, we must perish in dirt and filth. . . . We die in silence, in the stoke-hold. We see the sea breaking in through the cracked hull. We can no longer go up and out. We are caught. The steam hisses down upon us out of cracked pipes. Furnace doors have opened and the live coal is on us, scorching what is left of us. We hope and pray that the boiler will explode to make it short and sure" (p.119).

Greed is the propelling force behind civilization; all economic systems, not only capitalist ones, are included in Traven's indictment. "The deplorable thing, the most deplorable thing, is that the people who were tortured yesterday, torture today. The communists in Russia are no less despotic than the fascists in Italy or the textile-mill magnates in America" (p. 80). Traven blames World War I for an upsurge of nationalist feeling and a proliferation of bureaucracy: "All the world over, in consequence of the war for democracy, and for fear of communistic ideas, the bureaucrat has become the new czar who rules with more omnipotence than God the Almighty ever had, denying the birth of a living person if the birth-certificate cannot be produced, and making it impossible for a human being to move freely without a permit properly stamped and signed" (p. 201). Traven sees exploitation as a fact of life in all civilized societies; the *Yorikke*, he jests, may have once been a slave galley. But modern nationalism has produced more homeless and unemployed men than ever before, and the death ships exist to turn these "waste products" to economic advantage. Traven's social and political analysis is simplistic in its exaggeration and failure to draw distinctions; his ideas are secondary to the power of his symbols and narrative.

Yet most of the sparse criticism of the book dwells on Traven's social and political ideas. In one of the few essays that attempt to analyze Traven's main themes, H. R. Hays finds the central theme of *The Death Ship* to be the "proletarian as the disinherited man."[10] Granville Hicks welcomes Traven to the "great tradition" because in this and his other novels he speaks "always and in every slightest phrase as a class-conscious worker."[11] Hicks does have a point if we translate his statement to mean that Traven always identifies with the underdog. Traven is class-conscious, but he is hardly a Marxist, as Hicks would have us believe. Traven is a romantic yearning for preindustrial times, a kind of anarchist. The essence of his radicalism is expressed in the powerful central image of the book: nameless workers stoking the engines of the modern industrial economy. His power derives from his vision of life at the bottom of the stokehold.

This vision culminates in the sinking of the *Empress*. The shipwreck symbolizes the decline of the West brought about by the sheer weight of its greed and corruption. That Western civilization is sailing toward its death is clear to the underdogs of society, since they are in the vanguard of the journey. The *Empress*, the doomed new ship whose fate belies its appearance, represents the modern industrial state. The climactic fantasy of the wreck is Traven's vision of the destruction of that state resulting from its exploitation of the workers.

A comparison between Traven's sea story and Conrad's work is inevitable. Although both are writing in the same nebulous genre, their viewpoints are directly opposed: Traven sees life from the bottom of the stokehold; Conrad's point of view is generally from the bridge. There is an explicit allusion to Conrad as "that heavenly, that highly praised, that greatest sea-story writer of all time [who] knew how to write well only about brave skippers, dishonored lords, unearthly gentlemen of the sea, and of the ports, the islands, and the sea-coasts; but the crew is always cowardly, always near mutiny, lazy, rotten, stinking, without any higher ideals or fine ambitions" (p. 108). Traven's distortion of Conrad nearly cancels out his praise of him; Traven suggests that his own narrative is somehow more balanced and realistic. At the beginning of *The Death Ship* Gales insists that the "song of the real and genuine hero of the sea has never yet been sung" (p. 8) and that his story of "just a plain deck hand" will be a "true story of the sea [that] is anything but pleasant or romantic" (p. 8). Traven's insistence on the "truth" of a work belongs to the same romantic tradition as *Moby-Dick*, and may result in part from his having undergone the same general experiences as his narrator. He tries to justify the novel's ending, for example, by saying that "whoever could write another conclusion has never been a solitary shipwreck who has just had his last comrade washed over-board."[12] His novel is more realistic than Conrad's in the social sense, but not in the literary sense. What Traven fails to see is that although the events upon which the novel is based are real they are turned into symbols by his imagination. Not everyone would see a stokehold as an inferno, or a tramp steamer as a contemporary *Pequod*.

That Traven's reasons for being uncharitable to Conrad go deeper than resentment of Conrad's class perspective is suggested in his scathingly sarcastic allusions to O'Neill: "the hairy apes are opera-singers looking for a piece of lingerie" (p. 8); "There were no hairy apes around with lurking strains of philosophy for stage purposes. No time for thinking and looking under dames' skirts. Five seconds lost thinking of anything else but your stoke-hold might cause twenty square inches of your sound flesh to be burned away" (p. 149). Since Gales, who is supposed to be an ordinary deck hand, has his own "lurking strains of philosophy," the injustice to O'Neill is evident. Thematically, *The Hairy Ape* is closely related to *The Death Ship*. In O'Neill's play, too, an exploited coal stoker is identity-less and unrecognized by society. It is likely that Traven, a largely self-educated man, feels defensive about writing in the same genre as Conrad and O'Neill. He reacts by asserting that his own novel, a "romance of the sea" if ever there was one, is superior for its realism. Traven, like his narrator Gales, is sensitive to being questioned and reacts with gibes and exaggeration. Years later, in his conversations with Judy Stone, Traven was still criticizing these writers. He does say that "Conrad was a great writer," and that he particularly liked *Lord Jim*. But Conrad "never mentioned the ones who did the work." As for O'Neill, in *The Hairy Ape* "the sailors stand looking under the skirts."[13] Unlike Gales, who at least is grateful to those who help him, Traven is less than gracious to those who have aided him in finding his identity as a writer.[14]

Conrad's specific influence on *The Death Ship* seems to be derived chiefly from three of his stories: "The Heart of Darkness," "The Secret Sharer," and "The Brute." From "The Heart of Darkness" Traven may have derived the motif of a symbolic journey to the depths of the psyche. Both works deal with the disintegration of the protagonist's personality in the absence of civilization's restraints. In Traven's novel the horror of this disintegration is overshadowed by the final fantasy of the symbolic destruction of the West. There is no return to a white sepulchre of a city, nor is there a debt to society requiring the protagonist to make such a visit. "The Heart of Darkness" opens with symbolism which foreshadows an apocalyptic journey; both "The Secret Sharer" and *The Death Ship* open with a slight deviation from routine which has profound, unforeseeable consequences. The young captain's unusual act of taking the night watch himself in Conrad's story is roughly comparable to the *Tuscaloosa*'s premature sailing. Both stories then lead inexorably to a journey into the nonrational.

From the lesser-known story "The Brute," Traven may have derived the idea of the ship as a fearsome killer. Conrad refers to his ship, which has a reputation as an unpredictable man-killer, as a "big hearse."[15] His narrator describes the ship as being "mad": " 'Why couldn't there be something in her build, in her lines corresponding to—What's madness: Only something just a tiny bit wrong in the make of your brain. Why shouldn't there be a mad ship—I mean mad in a ship-like way, so that under no circumstances could you be sure she would do what any other sensible ship would naturally do for you.' "[16] Gales describes the *Yorikke* in strikingly similar terms: "Often an individual may be recognized as insane by his outward appearance. The more deranged his mind is, the more awkward or strange his way of dressing will be. . . . There was something wrong with the *Yorikke*. . . . Her appearance agreed perfectly with her mind, her soul, her spirit, and her behavior. Only an insane ship could look like that" (p. 86). Conrad's sailors, like Gales, at first vow not to sign on board: "They won't have me—not for double wages"; and "That's the . . . ship, Jack, that kills a man every voyage. I wouldn't sign in her—not for Joe, I wouldn't."[17] Gales says to himself that "even if I had a chance to escape the hangman by signing on for this bucket, I would prefer the hanging. . . . It was better to be a stranded sailor and hungry than to be a deck-hand on this ship" (p. 90). Both Conrad's sailors and Gales yield to the fascination of the brute ships by signing on for the perilous voyage. In the particulars of the voyage as well as in the overall conception, Conrad was clearly Traven's inspiration.

Traven's use of expressionism to heighten the story of a stoker's exploitation and betrayal shows his indebtedness to O'Neill's *Hairy Ape*. The extent of the debt may be reflected in the violence of his attack on a work in which expressionist distortion plays such a vital part. A basic problem in the critical treatment of expressionism is to determine whether the distortion is induced by the author for expressive purposes, or whether it is supposed to be a reflection of the protagonist's disturbed mind. Neither alternative precludes the other, of course, but in *The Death Ship* most of the distortion originates in the mind of the narrator. The progression from expressionism lightened by wild comedy, through the grim inferno of the stokehold, to the final apocalyptic fantasy reflects the changing emotions of Gales. The very distortion stems from Gales's projection of his feelings as an illegitimate child onto society and the death ships. And the hallucinations and dream-like state at the close of the novel reflect both protagonist and author who, with their "last comrade washed overboard," have severed their final ties with the realities of civilization.

Traven's self-consciousness may be reflected in the abundance of his literary allusions. In addition to his debt to Conrad and O'Neill, there are allusions to Dante, Melville, and Shakespeare, and there are echoes of Kafka. Melville's influence pervades this *"Moby-Dick of the stokehold"*[18] in which the narrator alone has escaped to tell the story. Both the *Pequod* and the *Yorikke* are microcosms of society; their voyages are romances of the sea filled with naturalistic details. A primary parallel is the first-person narrative of Gales, who, like Ishmael, boasts in rich colloquial tones of never going to sea as an officer. Gales: "I second mate? No, sir. I was not mate on this can, not even bos'n. I was just a plain sailor. Deckhand you may say. You see, sir, to tell you the truth, full-fledged sailors aren't needed now" (p. 7); and Ishmael: "No, when I go to sea, I go as a simple sailor, right before the mast, plumb down into the forecastle, aloft there to the royal mast-head."[19] Both men engage the reader in a kind of dialogue. Gales's colloquial American English echoes that of his equally direct Yankee predecessor. Gales, like Ishmael, insists upon his rank, which separates him from much of the crew. He can relate, he says, only to fellow members of the "black gang": "Funny that even among the dead these fine distinctions of rank and class do not cease to exist" (p. 220). To his social superiors he has little more to say than "Yes, sir" and "No, sir."

Both Gales and Ishmael narrate stories which begin with a wild farce that contrasts sharply with the ensuing journey into blackness. In both, the comic beginnings may be a cover-up for the narrators' anxieties over their uncertain identities and roles. "Gales" may not have been the narrator's legal name, and Ishmael's real name is never revealed. Disguises are prominent in *The Death Ship* in which the entire crew signs on with aliases. On Traven's ship, as on Melville's *Fidèle* in *The Confidence-Man*, "rarely if ever did anybody reveal his real name" (p. 186).[20] Disguises are a necessary defense against a society that shows its lack of charity in refusing to recognize its orphaned underdogs. Ishmael tells nothing of his family background except for an episode involving a punishing stepmother, and Gales seems strangely uncertain about his own mother:

"Your mother still alive?"
"I think so. But I do not know for sure."
"You do not know for sure?"
"How can I know for sure, sir? While I was away, she changed her address several times. Perhaps she's married to somebody whose name I do not know." (P. 54)

Billy Budd is a possible influence, for Gales's reply seems to echo that of Melville's protagonist:

Asked by the officer . . . his place of birth, he replied, "Please, sir,
I don't know."
"Don't know where you were born? Who was your father?"
"God knows, sir."[21]

Traven, like Billy Budd, probably a by-blow, also preferred to be
regarded as "evidently no ignoble one."[22]

With their new names and roles, Ishmael and Gales-Pippip descend into an inferno. The descent marks the turning point of their
dramas. Both experience a baptism by fire which assures their survival; Ishmael swears off the hunt, and Gales is "reborn" beyond
punishment. The stokehold and the try-works are described in similar Dantean imagery. Gales:

> At the bottom . . . I saw the underworld. It was a smoke-filled hell,
> brightened up by darting spears of reddish light which seemed to dash
> out of different holes and disappear as suddenly as they had come. . . .
> As if he had been born out of this thick smoke, the naked shape of
> a human being stepped into the center of the hall. . . . [He] seized a
> long iron poker . . . stepped a pace forward, bent over, and suddenly
> it looked as if he were swallowed up by the sea of flames which en-
> wrapped him. (P. 139)

And Ishmael:

> Standing on [the try-works] were the Tartarean shapes of the pagan
> harpooneers. . . . With huge pronged poles they . . . stirred up the
> fires beneath, till the snaky flames darted, curling, out of the doors
> to catch them by the feet.[23]

Wit, particularly phallic wit, serve both Ishmael and Gales as defenses and gestures of defiance. Ishmael has Yojo and the whale's
"cassock," Gales has his disguise as Pippip and the erect tower of
the *Empress*. Both men compensate for their feelings of impotency
with their wit. Gales's humor, particularly in the first book, seems
to be an attempt to hide his anxiety at being exposed as illegitimate.
Both he and Ishmael intend their hyperbole, gibes, and puns as re-
jections of the values of civilization. The ultimate defenses of these
two orphans might be the very stories they tell in which the entire
civilization is condemned to annihilation. Traven may have seen

Moby-Dick as a fantasy of the type he himself was to write: a fantasy of a rejected outcast who avenges himself on society first by loosening his bonds to it, then by symbolically destroying it.

Traven makes no direct allusion to Kafka, who deals with the same basic theme of the little man lost in a bureaucratic maze. When Gales, like Joseph K., is awakened by the police, his comic protests make him seem closer to Chaplin's tramp: "leave me alone. I want to sleep. You heard me. Get out of here. Get away from that door or I'll sock you." I wish that bum would only open the door so that I could fire my shoe into his face. So they call the Dutch a quiet people!" (p. 34). Yet the similarity of the situation to Kafka's suggests that Traven may be deliberately parodying *The Trial*. When Gales is arraigned, the police magistrate's explanation of the law sounds like that of Kafka's court: "The law is that anybody picked up without papers must be imprisoned for six months. When he comes out, he is deported to his native country. Your native country cannot be determined, since your consul does not accept you as a citizen. Then we have to keep you here with us, whether we like it or not" (p. 38). The enforcement of the law paradoxically creates a nightmarish inversion of justice.

Other parallels with Kafka lack any suggestion of parody. Both authors begin their narratives with a slight deviation from routine: an alarm on the night bell, an unexpected knock at the door, or the loss of an identification card. What follows is a profound alienation from reality as well as from society, as a dream-like atmosphere shades into nightmare. Both death ship and law courts are pervaded by a schizoid state of living death. Traven's depiction of this limbo between life and death, this alienation from society and self, makes him seem as contemporary as Kafka. Gales and Joseph K. might have continued their lingering existence indefinitely: Kafka never finished *The Trial*, and Traven's ending is problematic. But Gales, significantly, does not suffer the loss of feeling typical of Kafka's protagonists; Gales's humor gives way to fear.

In addition to the stokehold-inferno parallels, Traven also found in Dante the depiction of a state of living death:

37

I did not die, and yet I lost life's breath:
imagine for yourself what I became
deprived at once of both my life and death.[24]

Dante, when he loses his breath in Cocytus, experiences a claustro-phobic, stifling feeling similar to that of Gales in the stokehold. The *Inferno* and *The Death Ship* deal with the power of the father; Traven's work, more specifically, deals with betrayal by the father. In both works the punishment undergone by the characters is de-scribed in grotesque, expressionistic imagery. For Gales, abandoning his former identity by signing aboard the death ship with a pseud-onym is an apocalyptic event described with allusions to the Bible, Dante, Shakespeare, and Melville. But perhaps Traven saw in Dante, Melville, and Conrad, who were fellow exiles and orphans (Dante through his father's remarriage), an affinity that compelled him to invoke these writers so often. Like Dante and Conrad, he wrote his works in exile from his native land. As Gales-Pippip, Traven de-picted himself as a castaway of the type present in Conrad's works, one who is cast up by the sea on alien shores. And Traven probably sensed that Melville saw himself as much an orphan as Ishmael—or Pip.

That *The Death Ship* has a fresh and unique quality, despite its wealth of literary allusions, is due in large part to the original lan-guage Traven creates for Gales. The prose style has been character-ized by Arthur Calder-Marshall: "The style is at the same time collo-quial and mannered. It is American 'as he was never spoke.' Bombast is deliberately used in order not to impress; rhetoric to minimize, not magnify, horror. Over-statement is employed consciously as a form of underwriting."[25] Just as the *Yorikke* has its own *lingua franca*, so Gales has his own idiom. A good example is the passage in which Gales, having rejected suicide, steels himself for survival on the death ship:

Damn it, damn it all, and devil and hell. Now, listen here, boy from Sconsin, that pest *Yorikke* cannot get you. Not you. And all the con-suls neither. Chin up and get at it. Swallow the filth and digest it. Quickest way to get rid of it. . . . All the filth is only outside. Don't let it go to your soul and spirit and your heart. Take the plunge head-first.... And now away from the railing and away from that beast that is after you. Kick him right in the pants. Sock it right in the swearhold. Spit it out, and do it well. Spitting out the filth you feel in your throat is all you can do now. But make a good job of it. Now back into your bunk. (P. 130)

Gales's language is a weapon. The verbs "swallow," "plunge," "kick," "sock," and "spit" show him to be nearly choking with hostility. Ahab's speech is often similarly full of aggression, as when he tells Starbuck in the "Quarter-Deck" episode that he would "strike, strike through the mask," "thrust through the wall," "wreak his hate" upon the whale, and, in a grandiose conceit, "strike the sun if it insulted me."[26] In the chapter following the "Quarter-Deck," Ahab's soliloquy with its colloquial phrasing recalls Gales's speech: "I will not say as schoolboys do to bullies,—Take some one of your own size; don't pommel *me*! No, ye've knocked me down, and I am up again; but *ye* have run and hidden. Come forth from behind your cotton bags! I have no long gun to reach ye. Come, Ahab's compliments to ye; come and see if ye can swerve me."[27] The powerful white whale has become a "bully," its terrifyingly blank white mask "cotton bags." Ahab's colloquial personification of the whale serves to reduce its strength. Gales's personification of the death ship as "pest *Yorikke*" and his own suicidal impulses as the "beast" similarly reduces vague terrors to the level of the familiar. Gales's language is Traven's substitute for the active self that in Melville controls the direction of the voyage, if not its outcome. Like Ahab, Gales is "up again" after being knocked down. But while the captain can say "Naught's an angle to the iron way!",[28] Gales can only tell himself: "Now back into your bunk."

The "beast" that is after Gales is pent-up rage directed toward himself, rather than toward the external world, as it is with Ahab. The previously cited passage shows Gales sputtering and choking with rage against the condition to which his illegitimacy and his own reaction to it has reduced him. Gales's first reaction to having his illegitimacy exposed was flight; at the same time he sought to protect himself against the constant questioning with humor. Since on the *Yorikke* further flight is impossible, humor is the only defensive process remaining. Because he is facing possible death and battling his own suicidal impulses, his humor is now hardly distinguishable from aggression. Gales's humor in the above passage is very close to Freud's favorite "gallows humor."[29] Freud analyzes the joke concerning the rogue who worries about catching a cold on the way to the gallows: "the situation that ought to drive the criminal to despair might rouse intense pity in us; but that pity is inhibited. . . . As a result . . . the expenditure on the pity . . . becomes unutilizable and we laugh it off."[30] Gales also fights against pitying himself as the condemned "criminal." With the energy saved by not weeping or yielding to his suicidal wishes, he persuades himself to struggle in language that is humorous in its extravagant overstatement.

A good example of Gales's own gallows humor is his remark to the fireman after a falling cast-iron funnel nearly crushes him:

> "Almost got me. I would have been well mashed up. Nothing would have remained for Judgment Day. Well, anyway, I wonder what these guys, sent out at Doomsday to collect all the dead and bring them before the Judge, are going to do with the sailors fallen overboard or shipped over the rail and eaten by the fishes bit by bit—by thousands of fishes? I would like to see how they settle this affair of collecting all the sailors out of a hundred thousand millions of fish bowels." (P. 232)

The grimness of his situation is balanced by the grotesque exaggeration and apocalyptic imagery of the jest. The specific fear that finds its outlet in this passage is Gales-Traven's fear of "vanishing from the living" (p. 118).[31] Gales expresses a curious pride in serving on a "model of a death ship": "And then there are death ships that make fish fodder everywhere. *Yorikke* made carcasses inside, outside, and everywhere" (p. 150). Since he himself chose to sign on the ship, his black humor keeps him from regretting his own action. Ultimately, the *Yorikke* is a symbol of the grim joke that death has become in Western civilization. In *The Death Ship* the greatest "Joke is on Death itself."[32]

Although the novel deals with betrayal and flight, its tone is one of triumph. Gales survives against all odds; the coal-drag, having seen life from the bottom of the stokehold, is still undefeated: "I won't give up and I won't give in. Not yet. Not to the ground port" (p. 279). Although Gales, despite his resolve, almost yields to his death wishes, the story itself, told in the "barbaric yawp of an under-dog,"[33] expresses defiance and a will to live. A major theme of the novel is the disintegration of the ego, but the technique, with its fus-ing of literary allusions and colloquial narrative and its carefully modulated change from satire to expressionistic nightmare to sea fantasy, represents integration and control. Traven may have left his protagonist on a raft, but safe in Mexico himself, he probably al-ready knew that Gales would reappear as narrator in other works. The ironic voice of the author was to appear next in the story of the underdogs who carry with them the greed and death impulses of their civilization on their gold hunt in the Sierra Madre mountains.

3

The Treasure
of the Sierra Madre:
Fear
"almost to madness"

In *The Treasure of the Sierra Madre* (1927) Traven deals directly with the disintegrative effects of greed and fear on the individual psyche. For this modern exemplum on the text Radix Malorum,[1] he employs the ancient theme of the three companions whose search for gold ends in death. The novel is also an exciting adventure narrative of the quest for fabled treasure in the wilderness of the Mexican Sierra Madre, as well as an acute psychological study of the paranoid breakdown of a personality.

Fred C. Dobbs, the protagonist, has been left jobless in Tampico by the collapse of the 1920s oil boom. He is another superfluous man, a less likeable version of Gales. The question that occupies him at the beginning of the novel is, as Traven ironically remarks, the "age-old problem which makes so many people forget all other thoughts and things. He worked his mind to answer the question: How can I get some money right now?"[2] The answer seems to be the gold hunt on which he embarks with Howard, a wise old prospector, and Curtin, another down-and-outer. But this gold hunt proves to be as thoroughly ironic a solution as that of Chaucer's "Pardoner's Tale," the best-known treatment of the theme.

Howard, who has made and lost many fortunes in gold, warns the other two men that "gold is a very devilish sort of a thing . . . it changes your character entirely. When you have it your soul is no longer the same as it was before. . . . You may have so much piled up that you can't carry it away; but, bet your blessed paradise, the more you have, the more you want to add, to make it just that much more. . . . You cease to distinguish between right and wrong. You can no longer see clearly what is good and what is bad. You lose your judgment. That's what it is" (p. 50). Howard's statement foreshadows the events of the novel. At this point Dobbs claims he would be satisfied with twenty thousand dollars worth of gold even if "there were still half a million bucks worth lying around howling to be picked up" (p. 51). But Howard goes on to stress the dangerous aspects of the situation: "going with a partner or two is dangerous. All the time murder's lurking about" (p. 52).

To illustrate the dangers of gold hunting, Howard tells the story of La Mina Agua Verde [The Green Water Mine]. The Spaniards' attempted exploitation of the mine resulted in their massacre by the brutalized Indian workers, and a curse on the gold of Agua Verde that affected American prospectors centuries later. Traven, throughout the novel, is concerned with Mexican history, particularly the Indians' attempts to preserve their way of life from the gold lusts of the Catholic Church and the Spanish rulers. But the immediate effect of Howard's story is to cause Dobbs to become fascinated by the mystery of prospecting for gold; he suddenly speaks to Curtin of "that eternal curse on gold which changes the soul of man in a second" (p. 68). Dobbs reveals how impressionable he is: "Never before had he had the idea that there was a curse connected with gold. Now he had the feeling that not he himself, but something inside him, the existence of which until now he had had no knowledge of, had spoken for him, using his voice. For a while he was rather uneasy, feeling that inside his mind there was a second person whom he had seen or heard for the first time" (p. 8). Without realizing it, he is expanding on Howard's previous remark about gold being a "devilish sort of thing." Dobbs has shown that he is susceptible even to the mere suggestion of a curse, and, in the wilderness, this "second person" in him will come to the fore. Significantly, the more prosaic-minded Curtin denies the existence of any such curse: "It isn't the gold that changes man, it is the power which gold gives to man that changes the soul of man" (p. 68).

The strange ability of gold to "change men's souls" is apparent as soon as the men begin to accumulate gold dust. They decide to divide the proceeds every night so that each partner can hide his share from the others. Howard explains: "To make off with all the goods, dirty trick as it would be against your partners, would seem, out here and under these conditions, rather the natural thing to do" (p. 92). Alone with each other in the tropical mountains with a growing fortune in gold, the men are bound together only by their common aim and their back-breaking labor. "They had in common only business relations. That they had combined their forces and brains and resources for no other reason than to make high profits was the factor which had prevented them from becoming true friends" (p. 88). When Dobbs is trapped in a collapsed tunnel, Curtin rescues him and Howard helps to revive him. Yet Dobbs wants to know why they saved him: "I was just thinking why the hell you fellers dragged me out of that hole? Your shares would have grown rather big if you'd left me where I was for five minutes longer" (p. 89). This remark, which almost prompts a fight between him and Curtin, is the first overt sign that Dobbs fears betrayal. It may also be the first sign that he is thinking of doing that which he projects onto his partners.

Howard, who has seen many men act this way while gold prospecting, thinks that Dobbs's only fault is that "he's a bit too greedy. . . . Otherwise he's a regular guy" (p. 213). In any event, the men, who have fought off an attack by bandits, must now face the long difficult march back to "civilization," the train junction of Durango. Howard, emphasizing the difficulty of the return journey, says, "Gold is of no use to anybody as long as it is not where he wants it" (p. 186). To dramatize the point he tells the story of Doña María, a Spanish woman who manages to have her great fortune in silver and gold brought safely to Mexico City, guarded by an armed convoy. But when in Mexico City Doña María entrusts her fortune to the care of the Spanish Viceroy, and she then disappears from her bed, a victim of the greedy Viceroy. The difficulties which

44

arise in the Sierra Madre, however, originate in the characters of the prospectors themselves. Howard, who has revived an Indian boy suffering from shock, is forced to accept the hospitality of the boy's father as repayment. Curtin and Dobbs leave with his share of the gold, agreeing to meet him in Durango, or, if he is further delayed, to deposit his share in a bank at Tampico. The two younger companions are left alone in the wilderness with a fortune, and without the mediating influence of the wiser and older man.

A confrontation occurs during the attempt to cross the high Sierra Madre passes. At night in camp Dobbs breaks out in a "bellowing laughter," explaining to Curtin: "This old jackass of a boneheaded mug hands over all his pay to us and lets us go off with it like that" (p. 235). When Curtin professes not to understand, Dobbs explains: "Well, to make it plain to a dumbhead like you, we take the load and go off. What is there so very special about that? Nothing new to you, I should say" (p. 235). Curtin is astounded both at Dobbs's plan and at the suggestion that he himself has entertained such thoughts. He replies that he will not let Dobbs take the old man's property: "He's worked like a slave, the old man has. And for him, old as he is, it was a harder task than for us, believe me. I may not respect many things in life, but I do respect most sincerely the money somebody has worked and slaved for honestly. And that's on the level" (p. 236). This eloquent plea for the sanctity of labor is sincere but ironic coming from the mouth of a gold prospector who is trying to amass great wealth quickly. Curtin's remarks are interpreted by Dobbs as Marxist, and rejected: "Hell, can your Bolshevik ideas. A soap-box always makes me sick. And to have to hear it even out here in the wilderness is the god-damned limit" (p. 236). Traven naturally sympathizes with Curtin's sincerity and proletarian viewpoint but does not share the accompanying optimistic faith in human nature and the possibility of a just society. He uses the cynical Dobbs to mock this optimism.

The center of interest is in the psychological element, not, as some critics maintain, in the social commentary of a proletarian author.[3] Traven is ironic in his handling of Curtin's fumbling yet sincere belief in the sanctity of labor. He provides a foil for Dobbs's unwitting revelation of the change in his own character:

> "You can't hide anything from me, brother. I know that for sometime you've had it in mind to bump me off at your earliest convenience and bury me somewhere out here in the bush like a dog, so that you can make off not only with the old man's stuff, but with mine into the bargain. Then having reached the port safely, you'll laugh like the devil to think how dumb the old man and I were not to have seen through your hellish schemes. I've known for a long time what was brewing. I'm wise to you, honey." (P. 237)

Dobbs's accusation, patently unjust, is explicable only in terms of his own thought processes. He has accused Curtin of planning to do exactly what he has thought of doing. In other words, he has transformed his own desires by projecting them onto his companion.[4]

Dobbs's paranoid delusion, and the fear engendered by it, lead to the novel's climax. One senses the approach of the inevitable murder as Curtin comprehends the real meaning of Dobbs's accusations and endures a day and night of watchful horror. Curtin realizes that "there would come a night when one of the two would kill the other for no other reason than to gain one night of sleep" (p. 240). He sees that "in situations like this, Dobbs was the stronger, because he would act upon his impulse and think afterwards" (p. 241). The reader's tension increases because his natural sympathy for the protagonist is opposed by the knowledge that Curtin is more deserving of sympathy. Curtin finally falls asleep after being awake almost constantly for twenty-four hours and Dobbs takes his gun from him. He tells Curtin, "Your funeral has come. Because I can't stand living in constant fear of you" (p. 243). Dobbs's delusions have advanced to the point where he even denies that he is going to murder Curtin: "I don't mean murder. I only want to free myself from you and your intention to kill me whenever I may not be looking" (p. 243). The reader is both relieved and horrified when Dobbs pushes and kicks Curtin "some hundred and fifty feet into the bush, then [shoots] him down without saying another word" (p. 245).

Ironically, the attempted murder, which Dobbs assumes to be successful, raises his fears to the level of sheer terror. Dobbs thinks that "he saw a huge red face in the fire that ate and swallowed the flames" (p. 245). In the dense foliage around the campfire "he imagined he saw human forms, and then he was sure he saw faces" (p. 248). The jungle air seems to become dense and "gloomy, as though in a dream" (p. 251). Dobbs becomes afraid of the eyes of the burros, thinking that "perhaps Curtin might glare at him with eyes exactly like those of the animals" (p. 252). He decides that it would be better to bury him, but he "can't look at his eyes" (p. 252). Curtin is actually only wounded; unknown to Dobbs, he crawls through the bush and is rescued by an Indian charcoal burner who takes him to a village where he is nursed back to health by Howard. When Dobbs returns to the spot where he had shot Curtin, he finds nothing. When Dobbs returns to the camp, the burros "with their great black eyes" (p. 254) torment him; "for a second he thought he would blindfold them to be safe from these terrifying looks" (p. 254). Thus the paranoid fear of Dobbs's companion continues even in his absence and after his presumed murder. Dobbs's feelings about his victim are projected onto the burros. As substitutes for the slain man, they evoke much the same dread and awe. They have become totem animals in which the victim is symbolically resurrected.[5]

Dobbs's failure to find Curtin's body increases his confusion: "He tried to convince himself that it was not fear that tortured him, that it was nothing but the heat and exhaustion. Without forming words he babbled to himself that he was not afraid, that he was afraid of nothing, that he was only excited by the aimless running about and the vain search" (pp. 253–54). In his attempt to remove the object of his fears, he has created an external situation that justifies his fears. Yet the source is still his psyche. As in *The Death Ship*, Traven is concerned with the disintegration of the psyche in the absence of civilization and its restraints. But the fear, caused by society in *The Death Ship*, here stems directly from the individual. Dobbs, not society, is guilty of betrayal.

That Traven realizes the true meaning of his novels is well illustrated in this passage from a letter to an early admirer, the critic Manfred George: "I can't shake anything out of my sleeve. . . . I have to know the humans I tell about. They must have been my friends or companions or adversaries or my neighbors or my fellow citizens if I am to describe them. I must have seen the things, landscapes and persons myself before I can bring them to life in my work. It is necessary for me to have been afraid almost to madness before I can describe terror."[6] At the end of the passage, in a display of self-insight and openness rare for any author, but especially for the secretive Traven, he admits that the "friend or companion or adversary" he is describing in Fred C. Dobbs is himself. Fear almost to madness, and the mistaking of a friend or companion for an adversary, is the subject of *The Treasure of the Sierra Madre*.

Dobbs has yet to pay the full price for his betrayal. He has some moments of peace when his fear abates as he leads the burros within sight of Durango: "Here, in full view of the plain, he found real tranquillity" (p. 259). But Traven is lulling Dobbs into a false sense of security and prolonging the suspense as the ironic retribution approaches. Dobbs pulls the burros over to the side of the road for a rest; he hears someone say: "Tiene un cigarro, hombre? Have you got a cigarette?" (p. 263). Traven has emphasized the stillness of the tropics, and there has been an absence of dialogue since the shooting. For the reader as well as for Dobbs, "This was the first human voice he had heard for days, and it came to his ears with a shock" (p. 263). Dobbs realizes that he has made a mistake in pulling over to the side of the road, but it is too late. "Three ragged tramps" (p. 264) murder him for his valuable burros and animal hides with a blow of a machete. The bags of yellowish dust, slit open in a fruitless quest for something of value, are worthless to them. The gold dust, the object of the long quest, the cause of brutal labor and privation, and eventually of fear and death, is

48

blown away by the wind. The three thieves are captured by Indians when they try to sell the burros, and then executed by Federal troops.

In this sardonic tale, the three companions, in their differing attitudes toward gold, represent three aspects of personality. All are motivated by a desire for gold, for it represents freedom from constant need and an escape from their low status. But it is Howard who makes the crucial decisions of the search, and only he knows how to recognize the gold: "You two are so dumb that you don't even see the millions when treading upon them with your own feet" (p. 78). Only he knows how to survive in the wilderness: "Dobbs and Curtin would ask themselves earnestly what they would have done in this wilderness without him. They could have met with a field rich with fifty ounces to the ton of raw dirt and not have known what to do with it, how to get it out, or how to keep alive until time to carry it home" (p. 81). Howard tests reality, makes plans, and at the end decides that both he and Curtin will live their lives as medicine men to the Indians. Howard represents a strong sense of self. Curtin, whose name suggests a shadowy presence, is less individually characterized than the other two men. In the exchange previously quoted he is opposed to depriving another of the results of his labor. A spokesman for the dignity of labor and the rights of the worker, he speaks for the moral conscience; he tries to prevent Dobbs from stealing Howard's gold and is unable to murder Dobbs even when it is clear that if he does not, Dobbs will murder him. Dobbs lacks both Curtin's moral sense and Howard's sense of self. If Howard is the character we wish to emulate, Dobbs is the one we fear we might become. Dobbs represents more than the unrestrained lust for gold; he represents the forbidden wishes and impulses that we cannot think of without experiencing guilt and fearing punishment.

In the Stone interview Traven said that "*The Treasure of the Sierra Madre* . . . is the real autobiographical novel, whereas all the others are not." This statement tends to confirm the identification of the author with Dobbs in his "fear almost to madness." Later, however, "Croves" amended his words: "Only one of all the novels could be classified as a *biographic* novel, not an *auto*biography, but a biographic novel. One of the main characteristics of BT is in it, but let the reader find out who it might be."[7] Traven, of course, was being wilfully obscure in this interview, although he did seem to want to talk about his books. The latter statement could mean that *The Treasure of the Sierra Madre* is the biographic novel in that it describes three men who, taken together, represent the author's total personality.

Traven may have written a modern exemplum analogous to Chaucer's "Pardoner's Tale,"[8] but Traven's tale has another moral that is found in the epigraph:

> The treasure which you think not worth taking trouble and pains to find, this one alone is the real treasure you are longing for all your life. The glittering treasure you are hunting for day and night lies buried on the other side of that hill yonder. (P. iii)

The "real treasure" is the self, to be found in a real goal such as healing the Indians. Perhaps Howard's adopting the profession of "medicine man" is an implausible ending, but it is a symbolic alternative to the perpetual hunt for illusory treasure.[9]

The penalty for confusing the real and illusory treasures is either the dissolution of self undergone by Dobbs or a perpetual search for wealth as in the case of a fourth prospector, Lacaud. Lacaud follows Curtin back to the camp of the three companions, who decide not to kill him when they find out he is interested in an undiscovered lode worth "millions" rather than in their gold. Howard calls him an "eternal prospector," one who "can stay for ten years at the same place digging and digging, convinced that he is on the right spot and that there can be no mistake about it" (p. 178). He is "of the same family as were men in bygone centuries who spent their whole lives and all their money trying to find the formula for producing gold by mixing metals and chemicals—smelting them, cooking them, and brewing them until they themselves turned insane" (p. 179). He is a modern alchemist. The three companions leave Lacaud, who is still convinced of the reality of the fabulous lode. In "falsifying metals," he has falsified himself in pursuit of an illusory goal. So, by extension, have the other men.

The severe penalty paid by Dobbs is the loss of self. His beheading by the thieves is a punishment that fits the offense: he literally loses his head after having lost it from fear. Like Gales at the end of *The Death Ship*, Dobbs loses control over his actions and loses contact with reality; he becomes the victim of his fears. His end is foreshadowed by the story of Doña María who, just when she thought she was safe, "disappeared and was never seen again or heard of" (p. 209). She "lay down in her queenly bed, but since she did so, no one has ever seen her or heard of her. She disappeared mysteriously, and nobody knew what had become of her" (p. 209). Dobbs had "disappeared" even before his murder by losing control of himself. The fear of disappearance or loss of self lies behind both the paranoid breakdown described in this book and the strange state of living death described in *The Death Ship*. It is related to the deepest fears of an author who disappeared during his lifetime by remaining anonymous.

The theme of disappearance of self and the closely related theme of identity are in turn connected with the motif of descent into the womb. Gales's descent into the stokehold in *The Death Ship* appears here as a descent into the Sierra Madre, the Mountains of the Mother. Dobbs, who unlike Gales is actually guilty of betrayal, experiences death instead of rebirth. The treasure hunt is, as Freud suggested to Marie Bonaparte, a disguised womb fantasy: "there must be, in the unconscious, a connection between tales of seeking or finding treasure and some other fact or situation in the history of the race. . . . The 'buried treasure' in such cases would then be the finding of an embryo or foetus."[10] In gouging the gold out of the bowels of the earth the three companions have sought to rob the Mountains of the Mother of their treasure. The three mestizo thieves, on the other hand, help to restore to the earth what is rightfully hers. Dobbs, who has compounded the crime by betraying his comrades, is the sacrificial victim claimed by the earth.

Traven's story illustrates Bonaparte's theories in several interesting ways. First, there is the idea of the earth as the mother's body: "The earth, which bears and feeds us like the mother, in time becomes the concrete symbol of a vast mother."[11] The very name "Sierra Madre" shows that the gold-bearing earth is seen as a representation of the mother. Freud thought that tales of finding a treasure, such as Poe's "The Gold Bug," might be connected with a time in the "history of the race . . . when sacrifice was common and human sacrifice at that."[12] Dobbs may represent just this "human sacrifice." Poe's story and Traven's novel have in common the sacrificial victim and the mythical quality of the treasure hunt. "The Gold Bug" may or may not have been an influence on Traven, but the connection between gold and death is archetypal; Chaucer's "Pardoner's Tale" also links gold and death. If robbing the earth of its treasure is equivalent, in the unconscious, to robbing the mother of her child, then this act cannot go unpunished. The equation of the earth's treasure with the child is traced by Bonaparte to the infantile linking of feces and fetus and the mythological linking of feces and gold. She cites a Babylonian inscription defining gold as the "excrement of hell."[13] There is a hint of the latter connection in Traven's story when the gold seekers are placed, at least implicitly, in the eighth circle of hell, the place of Dante's alchemists.

The significance of this repeated pattern of descent into the womb remains to be explored. Traven's next novel, *The Bridge in the Jungle*, represents the culmination of this motif. In *The Treasure of the Sierra Madre*, as in *The Death Ship*, the motif is related to the problem of identity. Dobbs, unlike Gales, comes from a society where he had never had a meaningful job. Gales sees in the *Yorikke* an opportunity to find a new identity; Dobbs sees in the Sierra Madre only a chance to satisfy his lust for gold. Unlike Gales, who rejects the society that fails to recognize him, Dobbs brings the values of his predatory society into the wilderness. Dobbs is a cynical, amoral, snarling underdog. Trapped by the collapse of the oil boom in Tampico and without a job, he panhandles a few pesos for food and a room at the Oso Negro Hotel.

There, for fifty centavos a night, he has a cot in a tin shanty shared with other men. When he registers in the hotel, he uses the name of "Lobbs" for no apparent reason. But the clerk has not caught the name; in the register he writes "Jobbs." The irony is keen, for a job is precisely what Dobbs lacks. When he and Curtin manage to get a job setting up an oil rigging camp in the jungle, the contractor attempts to deprive them of their wages. Only by threatening him when they catch him in Tampico do they succeed in collecting the balance of their wages. In the wilderness, when Dobbs attempts to cheat Howard and Curtin out of the benefit of their labor, he is treating them as he has been treated.

Dobbs is murdered by men of his own kind. He at once recognizes the three ragged tramps as outcasts of society. As mestizos, half-Indian, half-Spanish, they belong neither to the agrarian society of the Indians nor to the commercial society of the Spanish. They are "types that are frequently met on the roads in the vicinity of cities, where they can sleep free of charge and wait for any opportunities the road may offer. Their look alone gave evidence that they had not worked for months and had reached the state where they no longer cared about finding a job, having tried in vain a thousand times. They were the human sweepings of the cities, left on the dumps of civilization" (p. 264). "Seeing these three empty tin cans of modern civilization, Dobbs, once in his life having been one of them himself" (p. 264), knows that he is in trouble. Dobbs, the mestizos, and the men of the death ships are waste products of modern industrial civilization, and those whom society despises often have no respect for each other.

Traven must have felt himself to be, at one time, one of these waste products of civilization. Like Dobbs, he had worked in the oil fields near Tampico where, as he told Luis Spota, he was called "The Swede." This epithet so upset him that he "decided not to use [the] name 'Torsvan,' typically Scandinavian."[14] His "true self" and his illegitimacy could not be hidden even in a strange land. Like Dobbs, he must have feared that others were "seeing right through him," that they knew he had no right to use the name of his "Scandinavian" father. Through his fictional counterpart he flees to the Sierra Madre, but the return to the womb means death. Dobbs's death is justified because of his betrayal of the mother; this is the crime committed by Traven's father in not marrying his mother. Dobbs, as the one who is left with the entire treasure, bears the ultimate responsibility for ripping the gold from the earth; he has caused its "separation" from the mother. Thus in his descent into the womb Dobbs does not find a surrogate identity but only an anonymous death.

In this "biographic" novel Traven is also represented by Howard. The old prospector who leads the way to the treasure foresees the fatal ending of the quest. He is at once the Pardoner, the old man, and one of the three companions of Chaucer's tale. When he comes upon the treasure, he "laughed in a satanical way" (p. 78) that suggests the Pardoner. At the end, when the Indians inform him that "only the sand is gone, of course," he "let out such a roar of Homeric laughter that his companions thought him crazy" (p. 305). The gold that they had gouged out of the mountains at such sacrifice is scattered over the ground by the bandits and carried away by the wind. He laughs again, this time joined by the Indians. He tells the puzzled Curtin: "Anyway, I think it's a very good joke —a good one played on us and on the bandits by the Lord or by fate or by nature, whichever you prefer. And whoever or whatever played it certainly had a good sense of humor. The gold has gone back where we got it" (p. 305). His laughter points up the cosmic absurdity of the quest.

Howard had always felt that ripping the treasure from the earth was an impious act. When the three men are ready to leave the mine, he insists that they restore the landscape. When the other two complain that it is a waste of time, he says:

> "The Lord might have said it's only a waste of time to build this earth, if it was He who actually did it. I figure we should be thankful to the mountain which has rewarded our labor so generously. . . . We have wounded this mountain and I think it is our duty to close its wounds. The silent beauty of this place deserves our respect. Besides, I want to

54

think of this place the way we found it and not as it has been while we were taking away its treasures, which this same mountain guarded for millions of years. I couldn't sleep well thinking I had left the mountain looking like a junkyard. I'm sorry we can't do this restoration perfectly—that we can do no better than show our good intention and our gratitude." (PP. 180–81)

Howard sees the gold-yielding earth much as Freud and Bonaparte do: as a mother deprived of her treasure. The tale ends with the mountain reclaiming its treasure, so that the restoration is perfect after all.

His feeling for nature and his ability to see the gold hunt in a larger perspective enable Howard to feel at home with the primitive Indians of the Sierra Madre. His role as healer and medicine man is a disengagement from Western civilization as complete as that represented by the wreck of the death ships. But here it is a positive act, not an escape fantasy. Some of the characteristics of the Indian way that appeal to Howard-Traven appear in the story of Doña María.

In the story of Doña María an Indian chief who knows of a fabled mine, but does not work it, tells an amazed Spanish friend that "I do not need gold nor do I want silver" (p. 194). The chief has the love of his wife and son and his fertile fields; "gold and silver do not carry any blessing" (p. 194). Whites, on the other hand, "kill and rob and cheat and betray for gold. You hate each other for gold, while you never can buy love with gold" (p. 194). The Indians know the real value of gold, for it is "pretty and it stays pretty, and therefore we use it to adorn our gods and our women" (p. 194). They understand the meaning of Traven's epigraph, that gold is the illusory treasure; love and a life close to the soil are the meaningful one. "I have a golden sun above me, at night a silver moon, and there is peace in the land. So what could gold mean to me?" (p. 194). And, finally, the Indians are always "the masters of our gold, never its slaves" (p. 194).

After Howard has brought the little Indian boy out of shock, he rejoins his companions. The Indians have not had a chance to thank him. So, the next morning, they catch up with the three men, who are in a hurry to get the gold dust safely to the rail terminal, and insist that Howard, at least, remain as their guest. To Howard's plea that he has business to take care of, the father of the rescued boy replies: "What is business, after all? Just hustle and worry. Business can wait. There is no business in this world which is urgent, señores. Urgent business is nothing but sheer imagination. Death finishes the most important and the most urgent business in a second. . . . There is always a mañana, always a tomorrow, which is just as good as today" (p. 226). The Indians honestly cannot understand this concept of "business" which is foreign to their beliefs. Indeed, the two seem irreconcilable. The boy's father says that his wife, who has been up since early in the morning making tamales, will "die of shame, thinking you believe her a bad cook" (p. 227). His description of the hunting, the Saturday night dances, and the pretty girls seems attractive, and his logic seems impeccable: "There is only one business on earth, and that is to live and be happy. What greater thing can you gain from life than happiness?" (p. 228). Howard cannot explain the concept of business to them. Traven ironically remarks: "Howard had no means and no words with which to explain to these simple men that business is the only real thing in life, that it is heaven and paradise and all the happiness of a good Rotarian. These Indians were still living in a semi-civilized state, with little hope of improvement within the next hundred years" (p. 228).

Nature, and the Mexicans, are proven correct at the end of the narrative. Traven obviously sympathizes with the three thieves who understand the value of Dobbs's burros, hides, tools, and clothing, but not of the little bags of sand: "Sand. Nothing but plain sand. Now, what did he carry this sand for?" (p. 274). The thieves debate the matter for a while and finally one suggests: "He knew that the hides are sold by their weight, and he was such a dirty cheat that he put these little bags between the hides to make them weigh more. . . . Well, I think we've spoiled his dirty business and saved a poor tanner's hard-earned money" (p. 275). After they slit open the bags, nature cooperates: "Then came the night breeze which carried all the sand, strewn about the ground, far and wide in all directions" (p. 276).

At the end of the novel Howard speaks to Curtin and reflects on the irony of a goldhunter becoming a medicine man:

> "Since I was robbed, I've been made into a great performer of miracles, a doctor whose fame is spreading all over the Sierra Madre. I have more successful cures to my credit than the best-paid doc in Los An. You've been killed twice and you are still alive, and will be, I hope, for sixty years to come. Dobbs has lost his head so completely that he can't use it any longer. And all this for a certain amount of gold which no one can locate and which could have been bought for three packages of cigarettes worth thirty centavos." (P. 306)

The novel concludes shortly after this passage, with Curtin recuperating and Howard being led away by the Indians to see other "patients." Having buried in the mountains the aspect of himself capable of betrayal, Traven rewards the stable side of himself with a happy life as a doctor among the Indians. The "miracles" Howard performs, the "successful cures to his credit," symbolize a degree of control over death.

Traven weaves stories of Mexico's legendary and historical past into his narrative, both to lend a mythical quality to the gold hunt and to show the effects of Spain and the Catholic church on Indian culture.[15] The stories of La Mina Agua Verde and Doña María are exciting narratives in themselves, but they also convey what Howard has called the "curse" on gold and demonstrate the rapacity and greed of the Spanish government and the Catholic church. The simple gold hunt becomes the quest of the Conquistadors for the legendary El Dorado.

While the four men are awaiting a bandit attack on their camp, Lacaud relates the third interpolated story, which concerns these same bandits. The bandits held up a train, murdering men, women, and children for their money and jewels. After they killed many passengers by firing into the compartments at point-blank range, they doused the cars with gasoline, immolating the survivors. Traven quotes them with relish: "With their war-cry: 'Viva nuestro rey Cristo! Long live our king Jesus!' the bandits had started the slaughter. With the same cry the long signal was given to begin plundering" (p. 137). Although the irony could scarcely be more obvious, Traven adds: "No better proof of what the Roman Catholic church in these countries had done to the people could be found than the fact that the same men who cried: 'Viva nuestro rey Cristo!' killed mercilessly and robbed for their own pockets men, women, and children whom they knew were members of the same church, believing at the time that they were doing so to help their church and to please the Holy Virgin and the Pope" (p. 143). As grotesque as the incident may seem, Traven is on firm historical ground, for similar massacres of innocents by lay Catholics occurred during the "Cristeros" rebellion of 1927.[16] In reaction to a decree by the Federal government banning priests from administering the sacraments, Catholics rose up and drove Federal troops from some rural areas. The result was more of the brutal warfare and banditry so common to Mexican history.[17]

Traven, who prefers the "feather-crowned god" of the Indians to the "blood-crowned god of the whites" (p. 193), seems to forget the ritual sacrifices of ancient Mexican religions. He is beginning to display what he calls the "influence of the atmosphere of the continent" (p. 85) by associating himself wholly with the Mexican spirit. His term recalls the "spirit of place" with which D. H. Lawrence is imbued when he looks forward to a resurrection of the feather-crowned god of the Indians in *The Plumed Serpent*. Traven praises the summary execution of captured bandits: "The final results are more effective than in countries where an average murder trial will cost around two hundred thousand dollars" (pp. 149–50). As for proof of the dead men's guilt, the officers "killed the rats first and afterwards looked them over to find out if they carried the pest" (p. 153).

Although he may approve of summary executions of bandits, they, no less than their victims, are underdogs and have his sympathy. He also has profound admiration and perhaps more than a touch of envy for their resignation before Fate. Bandits and soldiers will fight to the death, since "if you wish to survive, you have to win the battle" (p. 151). But if the bandits are not in a position to fight, they "shrug their shoulders and smile. They know that they are lost. But what does it matter? San Antonio, their patron in heaven, did not want to protect them, so what is the use battling against destiny?" (p. 148). After they dig their own graves, and smoke their cigarettes, they stand up in front of the graves. The captain asks, " 'Listo, muchachos? Ready, boys, for the trip?' Both answer with smiling lips: 'Si, coronel, yes, we are ready' " (p. 149). The writing is graphic, spare, and controlled as Traven portrays men who are in control of themselves in the face of death. Traven-Dobbs, who has felt a fear of death almost to madness, looks on with admiration.

The Treasure of the Sierra Madre may be characterized as an adventure narrative whose psychological depth distinguishes it from other books of the genre.[18] The voice of the author is cool and sardonic, his narrative ironic and controlled. Although the unstable Dobbs is the focus of narration, there is none of the distortion of *The Death Ship*. Traven eschews the expressionism and literary allusions of that novel to suit the genre of pulp fiction which he is using quite consciously. The novel contains a number of references to its genre. Curtin, after listening to Howard's story of La Mina Agua Verde, tells Dobbs that "there are a million such stories. Open any magazine and you will find them" (p. 68). When the two men return to the Oso Negro to tell Howard of their interest in gold prospecting, they find him "lying on his cot reading about bandits in a pulp" (p. 71). Later, the three men and Lacaud defend their camp from a bandit attack in a fast-paced, graphic episode in which Traven outdoes the pulp writers in their own genre.

The first page of the novel illustrates Traven's method of narration, which alternates between glimpses into Dobbs's mind, comments by the author, and, later, extensive dialogue. Traven begins by commenting that "the bench on which Dobbs was sitting was not so good. One of the slats was broken; the one next to it was

bent so that to have to sit on it was a sort of punishment" (p. 1).
Dobbs, however, does not notice the condition of the bench, for he
"was too much occupied with other thoughts to take any account
of how he was sitting" (p. 1). He is thinking of how to get some
money, and his thoughts lead him to panhandling, to rigging an oil
camp in the jungle, and to the gold hunt. Only in the first occupation does he receive money without becoming involved in cheating
and betrayal. The terse, ironic tone that pervades the author's comments and the protagonist's mind is suited perfectly to the action
of the novel. Traven identifies with Dobbs and his futile attempts
to earn money, and as long as he is alive that character is the focus
of Traven's sympathy.

Dobbs's disintegration, at least in the dramatic moments leading
up to the shooting of Curtin, is described for the most part in dialogue. The reader deduces Dobbs's paranoia from his words and his
laughter, comparing his distorted interpretation of the events with
Curtin's and Traven's relatively objective viewpoints. In the previously quoted passages where Dobbs accuses Curtin of planning to
steal all the gold for himself, he is obviously projecting. Dobbs's
remarks ending with "I'm wise to you, honey" (p. 237) give both
the reader and Curtin a glimpse into the disintegration of Dobbs's
personality. The point of view switches momentarily to Curtin: "If
Dobbs could accuse his partner of such intentions, it was proof of
Dobbs's shabby character, now revealed in full for the first time. If
Dobbs had such thoughts, then Curtin must look out for his own
safety. Dobbs would not hesitate to try to get for himself all that
he accused Curtin of trying to get" (p. 238). Curtin understands
the full implications of Dobbs's paranoia. Dobbs, for his part,
realizes "that Curtin would play fair, whereas he knew that he
himself would not give the other a chance" (p. 240). Here Traven
shows the lucidity of a person whose paranoia affects his motivation and his analysis of others, but not his ability to appraise the
situation that his own misinterpretations have brought about. Curtin, too, understands that "in situations like this, Dobbs was the
stronger because he would act upon his impulse and think after-

wards" (p. 241). Curtin's estimate of Dobbs shortly proves to be correct when Dobbs attempts to murder him.

In the absence of Curtin, the glimpses into Dobbs's mind necessarily become more frequent; his fears and continuing projections are now central to the book. These insights are deeper and more frequent in the short period of time elapsing between his encounter with the three thieves and his murder. Traven is building up the identification with the protagonist to intensify the shock of his death.

When Dobbs tries to get his train of burros moving again, he notices the thieves looking at each other and realizes how dangerous his situation is:

> It flashed through his mind that he had seen many a movie in which the hero was trapped in a situation like this. But he realized at the same time that he could not remember one single picture in which the producer had not done his utmost to help the trapped hero out again to save the girl from the clutches of a bunch of villains. Before he could think of any of the tricks he had seen in the pictures by which the hero finally escaped, he felt, with a strange bitterness in his mouth, that this situation here was real. And whatever is real is different. No smart film-producer was on hand to open the trap with a good trick. (P. 267)

Traven acknowledges the influence of his predecessors, the writers of pulp fiction and the producers of cowboy and thriller movies. But, unlike the protagonists of the popular genres, Dobbs has no tricks, no way out of the trap. He reaches for his gun but it does not fire. He remembers, too late, that Curtin had unloaded it. All this passes through Dobbs's mind in "a short second . . . filled with such tension that Dobbs thought the whole world would explode" (p. 268). He again tries to find a way out: "Still before this same second came to an end, Dobbs's mind worked intensely to think of another means of defense" (p. 269). He tries to reach for a machete tied to the saddle of the nearest burro, but one of the thieves throws a stone that crashes against his forehead. Before he can get up, another thief reaches for the machete: "tigerlike he sprang at the fallen Dobbs, and with a short powerful stroke he cut off Dobbs's head" (p. 269). Abruptly the narration has shifted from the protagonist's mind to the author's cool and objective description of his murder. After the graphic description of the murder, Traven enters the mind of the murderer: "He stared at the machete. There was not much blood on it. He wondered why. But the stroke had been that of a master hand. He did not realize how good he was, how great an expert. He stepped to the nearest tree, rubbed the machete clean against the bark, then, wetting his fingers with his tongue, tested the edge and, satisfied with his inspection, pushed the machete back into its scabbard" (p. 269).

The next chapter begins with a witty speculation on the minds of burros, again in Traven's terse, ironic tone: "Dogs often show a real interest in what men do, even when the men in question are not their masters. Dogs even like to meddle in the affairs of men. Burros are less interested in men's personal doings; they mind their own business. That's the reason why donkeys are thought to have a definite leaning toward philosophy" (p. 270). The tension arising from Dobbs's murder is thus reduced; the narrative voice directs attention to the murderer, the burros, the capture and execution of the thieves, and finally to Curtin and Howard. The narrative becomes objective again and the point of view is that of a detached and omniscient author.

A potentially valuable insight into the germination of the novel is given by Granville Hicks: "the whole exciting story might, though Traven has never read Marx, be regarded as a commentary on a sentence in *Capital*. Marx, it will be remembered, emphatically states that gold is no exception to the labor theory of value."[19] According to Marx, the value of gold as a commodity is not intrinsic but is derived from the labor men undergo to obtain it. Dobbs, who believes that gold has a magic power of its own, can be seen as suffering from the delusion which Marx calls commodity fetishism.

Marx, although seeking to unmask the true source of wealth as labor, never denies that the amassing of wealth has been a necessary element in the achievement of human progress. Traven, on the other hand, seems to see progress itself as illusory. He idealizes primitive societies where things have value only because they are useful and commodities do not yet exist. For him, the accumulation of wealth is unambiguously negative and is linked to the death instinct.

When Howard says "gold is always very expensive, no matter how you get it or where you get it" (p. 171), he means that the price is paid not only in hard work but also in fear and possibly in death. Howard, having previously made and lost fortunes in gold, has always known that the goal is unattainable, that the "glittering treasure . . . lies buried on the other side of that hill yonder" [p. iii]. Traven suggests that no amount of work can make gold valuable, any more than the alchemists could make precious metals out of dross. Only an irrational civilization values what is, paradoxically, false or fool's gold, and work aimed at amassing wealth is doomed to result in self-alienation. *The Treasure of the Sierra Madre* suggests that the lust for gold is a disguised death instinct, an archetypal theme that gives Traven's adventure story its universality.

4

The
Bridge in the
Jungle:
Primitivism

Traven's first two major novels express his attempt at disengagement from Western civilization. In *The Death Ship* both America and Europe are represented as destroyed, although in a fantasy in which Gales has lost his grip on reality. In *The Treasure of the Sierra Madre*, the three gold hunters form a microcosm of the society they left behind. *The Bridge in the Jungle* (1929), in which Gales becomes involved with a primitive settlement of Mexican Indians, can be seen as another chapter in Traven's continuing fantasy of escape from Western civilization.

Gales goes on an alligator hunt along the banks of a tropical river and stays at an Indian village too insignificant to have a name or to appear on a map. This impoverished community becomes the setting for tragedy when a little Indian boy falls from a bridge for which an American oil company "had considered railings an unnecessary expense."[1] Gales abandons the alligator hunt and joins the mourners at the boy's funeral.[2]

As in *The Death Ship*, Gales is the narrator, but he is observer rather than protagonist; that role falls to "inexorable fate"[3] and to Señora Garcia, the bereaved mother of the little boy. The Indians are planning their Saturday night dance when the young mother discovers that her son is missing. Gales comments in the same apocalyptic language he used for his signing aboard the *Yorikke:* "It would be a wild and whirling dance, to be sure . . . at which the trumpets and fanfares of Judgment Day would blare" (p. 46).

As the mother's foreboding changes to certainty that the boy is dead, she is no longer called "Señora Garcia" but "the Garcia." She becomes the archetype of all suffering mothers, an Indian *mater dolorosa.* Her intuition confirms what Gales has suspected all along, that "the boy is in the river! The boy has been drowned!" (p. 66). The plaintive cries "of a primitive Indian woman bewailing the death of a loved one" (p. 72) stir the men to search the river for the body. The discovery of the body is magnificently described. Bonfires light the river and the bronzed faces of the crowd; and the bodies of the divers flash in the river. Perez, a charcoal burner by trade, returns the boy to his mother with "that pitiful sad look which only animals and primitive people possess" (p. 113). This is the climax, the discovery of what fate has wrought.

The Bridge in the Jungle is another novel centering around the archetypal pattern of descent followed by death or rebirth. In *The Death Ship* Gales descends to the hold of the ship to be reborn as Pippip, immune to punishment and released from bondage to society. Here it is Carlos, Gales's substitute, whose descent and recovery free Gales from almost unbearable fear. Carlos is recovered from the depths of the jungle river in fetal position: "little Carlosito, whose knees are seen before anything else. His knees protrude high above the rest of his body because they are bent in an unnatural angle so that the heels are only a few inches away from the small of his back. One might think that the kid has been sitting on his heels all during the time he was on the bottom" (pp. 112–13). Traven may have been influenced in this scene by Queequeg's rescue of Tashtego from the "Great Tun" of the whale's head. As in *Moby-Dick,* one Indian recovers another from the water in a symbolic "delivery." Perez has to brave the dangers of an alligator-infested jungle river to recover the body. Like Queequeg, he has to demonstrate "courage and great skill in obstetrics" in the "deliverance, or rather, delivery."[4] But when Perez gives the body to the Garcia, the boy is returned not as an Isolato, but as a newborn child to his mother.

The mother, conspicuously absent in the other novels, is here the central focus of the narrative. Yet through her symbolic presence Señora Garcia becomes more than a mere human being. *The Bridge in the Jungle* is the culmination of the major works of the motif of descent into the womb. The death ship *Yorikke* and the Mexican wilderness of the Sierra Madre, the womb symbols of the other works, are replaced by a more direct symbol—the mother herself. Since Carlos makes the journey rather than Gales himself, the latter's role is largely passive. Half of the book consists of Gales's close observation of the mother's fears and sorrows, and her reactions to the child's death. But Gales is more than an observer; he shares the intuitions and feelings of the primitive woman. He senses the wings of fate hovering over the clearing just before the mother begins to fear for her child; he thinks he hears a splash in the river just before Señora Garcia questions him about the boy's whereabouts; and each has the same foreboding of the death. When Gales walks across the bridge at night for the first time, his foot strikes the rim. "Had I walked a bit faster," he says, "I would undoubtedly have lost my balance on striking the rim and I would have tumbled over and into the river" (p. 29). A little later Señora Garcia explains how she knows the boy is in the river: "I stumbled against the rim. . . . When this happened to me, right then my first thought was that should the kid run so wildly and thoughtlessly across the bridge . . . there is every chance that he might tumble over the rim and fall into the river" (p. 67). Each has the same intuition because each identifies with the little boy.

The identification of Gales with the suffering mother seems to stem from a feminine aspect of the author's sensibility: "in the tortuous time in which the unwritten form of the book pressed toward the light and cried for redemption, I followed the unconscious impulses in the soul of a woman or mother, in all aspects fumbling in an obscure corridor under the earth, because the blood and soul of a mother is in me as a universal heritage." In the rest of this sentence Traven explains that as a critic led by his "manly instincts" he cannot "judge whether the 'soul and feelings of a mother' are represented clearly, genuinely, and intelligibly for every mother."[5] He postulates the idea of separate and distinct male and female instincts in every person as a "universal heritage." The mind of the author, which conceives, gestates, and gives birth to the book, contains a considerable element of the "female" principle. The comparison Traven makes between the creation of the book and a difficult childbirth alludes, perhaps unconsciously, to the climax of the novel in which the Indian divers, "fumbling in an obscure corridor" in the tropical river, recover the body of the boy in fetal position.

Since Gales is no longer the potential victim of death by drowning, the narrative does not deal explicitly with his compulsive fear of drowning. But in this work Gales fears mental collapse, which allies him more closely with Dobbs than with the ebullient narrator of *The Death Ship*. At the beginning of the novel Gales is traveling on a jungle trail and meets Sleigh, an American who later becomes his friend. Sleigh holds him up merely to deprive him temporarily of his gun.

> "Stick'm up, stranger!"
> "?"
> "Can't you hear, sap? Up with your fins. And you'd better snap into it!" (P. 1)

Sleigh promptly explains that since Gales is obviously a "greenie," he "might have slugged me just for fear of me. I know greenies like you who get dizzy in the tropics" (p. 3). Gales learns from Sleigh that he is just as likely as the next man to "fall victim to any sort of hallucination" and he decides to "guard against the jungle madness" (p. 4). Traven is ostensibly describing Gales's initiation as a "jungle hand," but the references to dizziness, hallucination, and jungle madness show Traven's real interest is in the psychic rather than the physical dangers that Gales faces in the jungle.

Gales is anxious about being the only gringo in the tiny Indian settlement. He is aware that to the Indians he is an outsider. When the pump master offers Sleigh tobacco to roll in a corn leaf, Indian-style, he says to Gales: "You wouldn't like our cigarettes. . . . Take one of these here, they'll suit your taste better. You gringos prefer to be fooled about real tobacco." He then offers Gales an American brand, assuring him that he "never smokes that sissy stuff" (p. 19). Sleigh, who is married to an Indian woman, and whose children speak the native tongue and some Spanish, but no English, is not a gringo. Gales, then, is alone even in this intimate community.

Gales's sense of isolation and susceptibility to "hallucinations" foreshadow the nearly uncontrollable fear he suffers during the climactic recovery of the body. Even before the boy is missing, Gales imagines that he sees "phantoms of dead Indians and strange animals" (p. 24) as he dozes off in Sleigh's hut. His fears arise with no apparent cause: "They all were Indians and if, superstitious as they were, they thought I might bring them or their children harm, they would sneak in and kill me, then throw me into the river; and before Sleigh returned, every trace of what had happened would have been washed away" (pp. 24–25). Traven emphasizes not the superstitiousness of the Indians, which Gales uses to justify his fears, but rather the fears themselves. Death by drowning, anony-mous death, and betrayal are the obsessions of all of Traven's pro-tagonists. The rising action of the book, leading to the discovery of the body, is directly related to the intensification of Gales's feelings about the boy. As the discovery of the body draws nearer, Gales's sense of guilt and fear of retribution are increasing. His reactions to it will determine whether he, like Dobbs, will yield to his paranoia and fall victim to "terror almost to madness."[6]

As the entire community stands on the banks of the river and on the bridge to witness the midnight ritual leading to the finding of the body, Gales fears that the Indians will blame him for the catastrophe:

> One, only one out of this crowd has to stand up at this moment, only one has to point his finger at me and yell: "Look at that man! Look at him! He is the white, who has not been invited to come here but he

came nevertheless. He is the guilty one. By his blue eyes and by his skin of the pale dead he has brought the wrath of our gods upon us poor people. He is a gringo. He has brought us misfortune and sorrows. . . . Look at his eyes and you will see that with those eyes he is poisoning our children and bewitching all of us!" (P. 105)

It is true that the Indians are superstitious and that their Christian religion is blended with ancient Aztec beliefs, but Traven constantly emphasizes their courtesy and gentleness. They use the word gringo as a descriptive term without the pejorative connotations it has for many Mexicans. They show no sign of suspicion. Gales's fears of being blamed for the death are irrational and stem from his own feelings of guilt. The words of accusation that he puts into the mouths of the Indians may be correct in his own mind: the gringo has brought death with him from his floating tomb of a civilization. The bridge without guard rails and the shoes with slippery soles are American. While Gales imagines these things, the Indians are completely absorbed in finding the body.

When the body is recovered it is apparent that Carlos was killed by striking his head against the bridge rather than by drowning. When Gales examines the body he sees a "thick bruise . . . above the left eyebrow. The nose and mouth were swollen and the upper jaw was partly smashed in" (p. 115). He also finds a "little hole in the back of his skull . . . caused by a fairly thick nail" from the bridge (p. 115). These details show that it was not the river, which is part of nature, that killed Carlos, but rather the bridge, which was put there by civilized man.

Gales is again stricken by fear:

> The whole incident became unbearable to me. I was caught by the same fear I had felt for a minute or two while the board was floating upon the water. Any second I expected to see all eyes fixed upon me as having been found guilty of magic or witchcraft and so responsible for the misfortune which had befallen that poor settlement of peaceful natives. (PP. 119–20)

Because he had forebodings of the death, Gales feels that he is indeed guilty of the accusation he anticipates:

69

For a long time I had known that the kid was dead, or unconscious and nearly dead, before he reached the water and that he was surely dead five minutes after I had heard the splash. No, after I had heard a fish jumping high into the air to catch a mouthful of mosquitoes. That splash had been caused by a fish. I would swear it was a fish. And I would stick to that story until the end of my life. I did not wish to be haunted all my life by the sound of the splash I had heard early that night. (P. 120)

In full view of the crowd he steps forward and asks to examine the body. He listens for the heartbeat, lifts the head, but feels the "repugnant coldness of death only that much more, and only that much more . . . realize[s] the helplessness of man against death" (p. 121). His action, which puts him in touch with reality, relieves him of his recurrent guilt and fear: "My fear had gone. That painful agony which had gripped me twice that night had disappeared entirely. By my careful examination of the kid's heart, useless though it was, I had shown that I was willing to help. So I had been accepted as one of the mourners" (p. 121). He is accepted as one of the mourners, his fears are assuaged, and he earns the right to weep at the funeral as if he had lost "my boy, my little brother, my fellow man" (p. 213).

Gales suffers from a fear of death by drowning that is as deep and compulsive as his fear of betrayal. Although Gales never mentions this fear in *The Bridge in the Jungle* and alludes only once in passing to the death ships, it is significant that little Carlos is a victim of the same death that had threatened Gales himself in the earlier novel. When Gales mourns the boy, he is mourning himself as he might have been were it not for his miraculous escape. When Gales-Traven describes the mother holding her dead little boy, he is describing his surrogate self being comforted in death. Perhaps this is why Gales's fears seem so out of keeping with the rest of the book, which is ostensibly a study of primitive life in which Gales merely serves as a sympathetic observer. In the strange logic of the unconscious, the Indian accusation of betrayal is justified because Gales-Traven is using the boy as a surrogate-victim or scapegoat to work out his fears. The Indians' slaying of the gringo as scapegoat would compensate for the "blue-eyed" Traven's using Carlos as a scapegoat.

Gales is as closely related to Dobbs as *The Bridge in the Jungle* is to *The Treasure of the Sierra Madre*. In *The Bridge in the Jungle* Gales tells the story of the recovery of a body from the jungle, as Traven had previously told of the recovery of gold from the mountains. Carlos, a true "child of the jungle" (p. 126), is a gift of the earth much like the gold in the earlier novel. When his body is recovered from the jungle river, Gales ties up the jaw of the corpse because the mother "wanted to have a beautiful dead baby" (p. 133). In helping to restore the battered body to its previous appearance, Gales acts much as Howard does when he restores the mountain to its former appearance. The Mexican wilderness regains its treasure.

The Treasure of the Sierra Madre ostensibly concerns the disintegrative effects of greed on the psyche, but on a deeper level it depicts fear and paranoia arising from the enactment of a birth fantasy. Significantly, the same terror almost to the point of madness afflicts Gales in the present novel at the moment when the body is discovered in fetal position. *The Bridge in the Jungle* shows the paranoia and the fear of death by drowning being put to rest by the return to the mother. This helps to explain the source of the fear and the meaning of the descent into the womb.

After his explanation of the origin of the book, Traven says: "It is *my* mother who grieves, it is *my* child, *my* brother, *my* heart and flesh and blood, that here stands defenseless and helpless before an inexorable fate."[7] The death and recovery of the body may be seen as a fantasy in which Gales-Traven gives himself the mother from whom he has been separated for so long, and as a fantasy in which "his mother" grieves for him in the form of the drowned child. But the third member of the fantasized family is Gales, not the father. The actual father in the novel is an ineffectual man, appreciably older than his young wife. When the body is found, the mother and the women of the community prepare the body for burial and arrange for the funeral. The men have no role in this process, and

71

Señor Garcia drowns his grief in mescal. A friend who is also drunk has to help him during the funeral procession. In the second half of the novel, after the recovery of the body, it is the mother's grief that provides the main interest. In denying the importance of paternity, Traven may be compensating for the initial "betrayal" of his mother by his father.

For the first time in Traven's works, and for the only time in his major works, a woman appears as an important character,[8] but only in the role of mother. She appears not in a sexual role, nor even as a mother bearing her child, but only as a womb to which the child returns in death. Gales-Traven's early separation from his mother has left him with a basic insecurity which makes it impossible for him to depict either women or himself in an adult relationship. Because he always depicts himself in his works as an abandoned child, he can depict women only as mothers.

The return to the mother seems both to resolve the problem of identity and to put to rest the fear of anonymous, unmourned death. Gales expresses his dread of anonymous death and disappearance when he suspects that the Indians may blame him for the catastrophe:

> If I never come back again, if I am sacrificed here and now, tonight, nobody, no consul, no ambassador, no government, will ever know what has become of me and where my bones are bleaching under the sun. The buzzards won't leave anything of me that could be identified. "Disappeared on a trip through the jungle." Or perhaps: "Caught by alligators on a fishing trip in swampy territory." This will be the last the old folks at home will hear of me. (PP. 105–6)

In the first novel he expresses a similar dread, although there the language is apocalyptic:

> I wonder what these guys, sent out at Doomsday to collect all the dead and bring them before the Judge, are going to do with the sailors fallen overboard or shipped over the rail and eaten by the fishes bit by bit—by thousands of fishes? I would like to see how they settle this affair of collecting all the sailors out of a hundred thousand millions of fish bowels.[9]

72

In both cases the fierce humor indicates repression of emotion. Behind the aggressive humor is the compulsive fear of loss of identity—the real terror behind the fear of death by drowning.

The fear of death is often aroused by "an experience of loss or threat of loss of the self-identity." In those whose fear of death has this origin, "loss of the ego and loss of life are equated."[10] Traven's insecurity, coupled with his compulsive fear of death by drowning, illustrates this. Drowning represents an anonymous, unmourned death in which, in Gales's grotesque metaphor, the self ends up in "fish bowels." Death is the complete annihilation of the ego; obsessive fear of death by drowning, then, is related to fear of becoming paranoid and fear of disintegration of the ego. Fear of death and fear of madness are "parallel phenomena in anxiety, both representing the fear of nothingness." Furthermore, the "dissolution of the unity of the personality is equivalent to vanishing or losing awareness of existing as a person."[11] When paranoia results in the disintegration of Dobbs's personality, he disappears as is symbolized by his beheading; Gales, aboard the *Yorikke*, fears that he has "vanished from the living."[12] In *The Bridge in the Jungle* the fear of death and the fear of madness are linked, and we see this in the attack of paranoia Gales experiences when the body of Carlos is found. When the body is returned to the mother, there is no longer the possibility of Gales's "vanishing or losing awareness of existing as a person."

Gales gives himself an identity through his surrogate victim. Little Carlos is mourned by his mother and his community whereas Gales, if he were to die, would simply "disappear on a trip through the jungle" (p. 106). The boy's connection with the mother establishes his origin and identity. Unlike Gales, who has only the vague "old folks at home," Carlos has a concrete familial identity. His loss of identity is only temporary and ends with the reappearance of his body. Little Carlos may have been "happy in his own way" (p. 197) at the bottom of the river, but Gales-Traven would not have been able to leave him there, anonymous and unmourned. His body had to be recovered and reunited with the mother.

The figure of the Garcia emerges out of Gales-Traven's deepest needs. Gales-Traven does not have to stop the "flutter of an unanswered question" with a lie, as Gales had done in the first novel, or as Traven was to do in his will. In this will, written three weeks before his death, Traven fused the three personalities he assumed during his lifetime by calling himself "Traven Torsvan Croves." The Spanish language enabled him to use as his legal surname the name he claimed was his mother's. In *The Bridge in the Jungle*, "Croves" becomes "Garcia" through Traven's identification with the mother. Torsvan, the father, is replaced by Gales himself. And Traven becomes "his child," little Carlos. It is no wonder that Traven considered *The Bridge in the Jungle* to be his "master work, difficult for any writer to surpass," as he told Luis Spota. He also said that "B. Traven knew it word for word."[13] Traven, like his narrator, must have often looked back to "those twenty-two hours when the Great Bandmaster was down on earth" (p. 211).

In one respect, however, even this wish-fulfilling fantasy is unsatisfactory. In denying the role of the father he does not answer the question: "Where is the foundling's father hidden?"[14] He constructs a fantasy in which he avoids another betrayal, but the question that drives him to the death ships and into the Mexican jungle remains. Not until the late short novel "Macario" will the missing father, in the guise of "Godfather Death," make his appearance.

Although Traven thought of *The Bridge in the Jungle* as his best novel, it is inferior to *The Death Ship* and *The Treasure of the Sierra Madre*. Since Gales plays a passive role in this drama, the psychological impact is lessened. Traven is at his best when the potential victim of his compulsive fears is his persona, Gales, or an alter ego such as Dobbs. The interest in the novel declines sharply after the body is found, because Gales has little left to do but comment on the natural grace, honesty, and decency of the Indian community. Traven himself may have thought of his novel primarily as a study of primitivism. In his essay on the novel he says that it was intended to show the Western reader the "deepest heart

74

sorrow of a non-white, of an Indian mother."[15] This social purpose is expressed in the Whitmanesque epigraph:

To the mothers
              of every nation
              of every people
              of every race
              of every color
              of every creed
              of all animals and birds
              of all creatures alive
                            on earth (P. iii)

In the Indian community death is a natural conclusion to a way of life instead of the grim joke it has become in Western society. Perhaps in this limited sense the book is a "pantheistic ode" as one critic has suggested.[16] Alfred Kazin treats it as primarily a study of primitivism: "[Traven] has tried to explain primitivism in its own terms, in the light of its ragged, dumb aspirations and through the cycle of appetites that is its custom: but he has succeeded not because he has penetrated native life with extraordinary brilliance, but because he is himself a glowing example of the soul-stricken urban man."[17] There are two scenes which describe the community's primitive rites. The first occurs at the halfway point of the novel when the child's body is located by means of an ancient rite consisting of floating a lighted board on the river. The board "rests quietly on the water as if it were deciding which way to go" (p. 102), and then, hearing the child "calling," it stops directly over the place where the body is.

With this "magic," the Indian community is for the moment recalled to its pre-Columbian past. The old Indian who remembers the ancient rite looks like one of the "old Indian priests of the ancient Aztecs and Toltecs" (p. 98). The influence of Western civilization and Christianity is stripped away:

If the old man had said: "Now I need the bleeding heart of one of you," half a dozen men and youngsters would have stepped forward

to offer it. . . . because they had lost their own free will and had become spellbound. None of them would offer his heart or even a hand to
please a Catholic priest. Their brujos and medicine men still held
immense power over their souls and minds—in most cases for their
own good. (P. 93)

Here at the "central point of all worldly and other-worldly
events,"[18] rational, scientific explanations give way to magical
ones. Like Jim's magic in the raft scenes of the *Adventures of
Huckleberry Finn*, the ancient rites of the Indians prove supreme.

Gales, of course, is skeptical. Even when the board starts to move
against the river's main current, he wonders "which of us, the crowd
or I, will be right in the end" (p. 109). Even when the body is
discovered at the exact spot where the board stops, he is not content with the evidence. Lacking a rational explanation for it but
unwilling to accept that of the Indians, he presses the phlegmatic
Sleigh for an answer to the mystery. But Sleigh is content without
a scientific explanation; it would be a waste of time, he tells Gales,
to relate other "strange things" he has seen while among the Indians, for "you don't believe in anything. You are one of the wise
guys. Why, I'm sure you don't even believe in ghosts. I do and I
could tell you lots about them. But what's the use with a guy like
you?" (p. 143). Gales makes one last attempt to find an explanation by asking Perez, the man who found the body, how the light
"knew" the body was there: "Nothing simpler than that, mister.
The kid was calling the light to come to him and show us the way.
So the light had to obey, and it came. There is nothing strange
about that. It's quite natural. Anyone can see that" (p. 148). Sleigh
laughs again and insists that there is no mystery, that the "Indians
can't practice any more magic than you can or me" (p. 148). Gales,
the only "civilized" man present in the community, gives up his
attempt to find an explanation.

The serio-comic, grotesque funeral that concludes the novel shows
the Indians adapting Christianity to their own way of life. After an
all-night wake, the entire village takes part in the funeral procession. They travel on a blazing hot jungle trail until they reach the

battered Catholic cemetery where the boy is to be buried. The Indian band plays American dance tunes, including that "great American *Te Deum*, Taintgonnarainnomo" (p. 193); four young boys carry the coffin while the father, drunk on mescal, supports an even drunker companion; when the procession arrives, the poverty-stricken village schoolteacher is almost too drunk to deliver the sermon. When he glances at the mother, however, the schoolteacher attempts to deliver his speech. Standing on the edge of the grave, he waves a twig in his right hand "as if he were going to fight an invisible enemy who is defending himself with a sword. . . . He apparently sees in this lake of faces a monster creeping towards him, because his features are distorted with terror" (p. 209). He tries to conquer his fear of this monster, Death, by shouting "the little boy is dead. He is completely dead. I am sure of that. We'll never see him again. We shall never, as long as this world may exist, never more hear his innocent and happy laughter" (p. 209). After speaking of the great sorrow of the mother, he strokes the air too energetically with the twig and tumbles into the grave. After a few moments he is rescued.

Renewed by this mock "death and rebirth," he shouts even louder: "The little boy had to die so soon. . . . The good little boy had to die so very soon, and he is dead. We have all loved him very much. We have been happy when he was with us. Now he is gone. For this we feel very sorry and blame none. It had to be. He is dead. Now we will bury him. Adiós, my little boy, adiosito!" (p. 212). The speech, tough-minded and uncompromising in its recognition of the finality of death, strikes a responsive chord in the audience. The entire community, including Gales now, "weeps and howls," but "it is no longer the shrieking of the night. It is a mournful weeping as if it were over something which had happened centuries ago and was now recalled to mind by a well-written narrative" (p. 212).

Traven makes it appear that Gales's catharsis comes at the same time as that of the community. If the novel were primarily a study of primitivism, the climax would be the funeral scene in which the sympathetic Westerner becomes a member of the community by mourning the death of one of its members. But *The Bridge in the Jungle* is of particular interest only when viewed in the context of Traven's obsession with identity and fear of disintegration. The true climax, then, comes halfway through the book with the recovery of the body and the reunion of the child with his mother. After that, Gales is a superfluous character; Traven may have found that he could best describe Indian life without a narrator, as he did later in the series of Jungle Novels.

5

The
Jungle
Novels:
Revolution

Traven's series of six Jungle Novels, written between 1931 and 1939, deals with the revolt of Indian laborers in the monterías [lumber camps].[1] The Indians, robbed of their land and culture by the Ladinos [Spanish Mexicans], are forced into the monterías and rise up in rebellion. These rebellions were part of the Mexican Revolution of 1910. Traven's sympathy for the Indians oppressed by the Diaz dictatorship is also a fascination with their torments, which are similar to those of Gales in *The Death Ship*.

The first three novels, *The Carreta*, *Government*, and *March to the Montería*, show the ignorant and illiterate Indians exploited by a government run by and for the Ladinos. Under the corrupt Diaz dictatorship they are either peons tied to land owned by Ladinos, or forced debt-laborers on plantations and monterías. The pivotal novel of the series, *The Rebellion of the Hanged*, begins with the initiation of an innocent into the vicious and corrupt system of debt labor. This is the same motif employed in *The Caretta* and *March to the Montería*. The innocent is Candido, an Indian who is thrown into debt when his wife has an appendicitis attack. She dies before he raises the money for medical expenses, but the Ladino doctor insists on being paid. Don Gabriel, the labor agent, pays Candido's debt and sells him at a huge profit to a montería, where he will work his debt off in two years, if he survives.

Here he joins Andrés and Celso, the protagonists of *March to the Montería*, who have already begun their servitude.

In the mahogany camps, each cutter must produce three tons of trimmed lumber daily. The penalty for not meeting the quota is hanging "from a tree by his four members, and even by five, for half the night."[2] If the worker dies,

> the Montellanos [the owners of the camp] and their bodyguards were not concerned . . . beyond the fact that a death affected them by meaning the loss of a man's labor. If a cutter was lazy or weak and could not produce three tons of mahogany daily, the loss was not great, the man could die quietly. For the worker, work is a duty. If he is lazy, he has no right to live. After all, if he dies, there is one less nuisance. (P. 111)

The Indians' fear of being hanged is a terror "to madness" (p. 113), like the fears of Gales and Dobbs. But this terror is merely named, not dramatized as in *The Treasure of the Sierra Madre*. Traven seems more interested in cataloging the horrors of the labor camps than in examining the psychological effects of these torments on the victims.

> "There's still another marvelous punishment. . . . Toward eleven o'clock in the morning they grab a man and take him to a place where there isn't a tree or any shade of any kind. They take off his clothes, tie his hands and feet, and bury him in the hot sand to just below his mouth, leaving only his nose, his eyes, and the top of his head aboveground, and all this under the caress of the sun." (P. 112)

The jungle monterías are explicitly compared to an inferno: "Here you're not just at the entrance to hell; here you're at its very bottom" (p. 103). The Indians, like the men aboard the death ships, are in the ninth circle of hell. They too have been betrayed by their government, stripped of their identity and condemned to hard labor. Just as Gales and his fellow crew members feel that they will be "beyond punishment" if they survive the stokehold, so the Indians, having survived burial alive and hanging, no longer have any fear of punishment. They develop a "revolutionary" song:

80

If my life is worth nothing
And I live worse than an animal,
I'd lose nothing by killing
Him who has hanged me,
And I'd gain a lot sending
A condemned man to hell.
Ay, ay, ay, ay, little iguana,
Let's go to the tomb to sing. (PP. 101–2)

They consider themselves "soldiers of the regiment of the hanged" (p. 94) who have nothing more to lose. From the tomb of the monterías they are reborn as revolutionaries.

Traven's compulsive fears are reflected in his depiction of the bloody acts that spark the revolt. The first act of rebellion is the blinding of Don Acacio, the most brutal of the Montellano brothers, by Urbano, the Indian he is about to flog for attempting to escape from the montería. Candido also attempts to escape. To punish him Don Felix, another Montellano brother, cuts off his ears and those of one of his sons. Candido's other son drowns in his father's futile attempt to escape. When Candido's sister Modesta is attacked by Don Felix, this is the final act which sets off the rebellion. Traven characterizes the Indians' bloody acts of revenge on the Montellanos as man's acting "like an animal, like a brute, trying to recover his human dignity" (p. 266). More interesting than Traven's explanation of revolutionary violence are his descriptions of the punishments and the Indians' revenge.

The attack on Don Acacio is the forerunner of the violence that follows. A close reading of Traven's description of the blinding suggests a possible source of his interest in this act of rebellion. Urbano, about to be flogged, is mesmerized by Don Acacio's whip: "The enormous whip wavered before Urbano's eyes and at times its tip seemed to strike the agitated water" (p. 148). The whip may be a phallic symbol, "enormous" to the "unmanned" Indian who is about to suffer the pain and humiliation of flogging.

Again Urbano looks at the whip and seems to see it as having a life of its own: "he saw the whip hanging from his torturer's wrist.

With an instinctive reflex movement he struck violently at his enemy's arm and knocked him against the tree. Don Acacio's head slammed against the trunk" (p. 152). After this almost involuntary blow the Indian is "guided more by terror than by his reflections and his dreams [of escape]. Terror drove him to carry out to its ends what he had begun" (p. 153). Don Acacio is tied to the tree and it is his turn to feel fear "for the first time in his life" (p. 160). "A shadow of cruelty crosses Urbano's eyes" (p. 159) as he picks up a mahogany branch "with thorns as long as a finger and as hard as steel" (p. 159). He flings himself at Don Acacio twice, striking his eyes out. Urbano, after being emasculated by the Ladinos all his life, has won back his manhood.[3] But he fears a horrible death as punishment for the attack and drowns himself. The helpless and humiliated Don Acacio shoots himself.

When the actual rebellion begins, the vengeance exacted on the two remaining Montellano brothers makes the symbolism of castration more obvious. Don Severo attempts to talk to the rebels, but they shout "Down with the Spaniards! Down with the white men!" (p. 271).

> He felt clumsy, not knowing what to do with his hands and arms. Finally he let them fall with a grotesque gesture, leaving them hanging in front of him as though trying to protect his lower belly, in the attitude of a schoolboy caught trying to satisfy an unhealthy desire. He did not realize how comic his position looked until the boys shouted at him: "Hold the little bird tight! Don't let it fly away!" (PP. 271–72)

Don Severo's gesture, which according to Traven looks like either an attempt to masturbate or to protect his phallus, is interpreted by the Indians in the latter way. They laugh and one of them shouts: "You can't save it, Spaniard! You won't be able to use it tonight!" The Indians charge at him and his foremen, shouting their rebel cry, "Land and Liberty!" (p. 272), the famous slogan associated with one of the heroes of the Mexican Revolution, Emiliano Zapata.[4] Don Severo and the foremen are pounded to death by the

Indians, "battered to pulp, torn to pieces. Their remains were brought back into the office by the boys, who immediately started to round up the pigs and dogs to shut them in with the corpses. Thus the carrion was devoured by the animals" (p. 274). They suffer the dreaded anonymous death which Traven reserved for those who deprive others of their identity.

The third brother, Don Felix, is captured alive in the Indians' attack on the camp headquarters. He is the one who had the ears of Candido and the ears of Candido's little son cut off, and who attempted to rape Modesta. Modesta, an Indian *mater dolorosa* who has been mourning the death of one of her little nephews and the maiming of the other, becomes a threatening harpy who, in a long tirade, condemns Don Felix to hell. He is hanged by one ear as an appropriate punishment. His pleas to the Indian boys to cut him down and kill him go unheeded, and he is left there to die an agonizing death.

The violent, often savage behavior of both Ladinos and Indians goes far beyond what is necessary to convey the idea that the Indians are cruelly oppressed and that they avenge themselves with equal cruelty. Traven himself seems to have realized that he lost control over his material in *The Rebellion of the Hanged*. He told Luis Spota: "If you read *The Rebellion of the Hanged* you will note that until page 30, the writing is truly notable; but, from there on, everything changes, so much that the author appears to have suffered a crisis, an infirmity, something abnormal.[5] Perhaps the crisis or infirmity suffered by the author is the recurrence of his obsessive fears. The indulgence in violence, instead of providing a release for these fears, may have served to aggravate them.

Traven dwells on death and maiming because they attract and repel him. In *The Death Ship*, it becomes apparent that Gales's professed "love" for the *Yorikke* is an attraction to the possibility of his own death. In the Jungle Novels Traven is preoccupied with violence in the specific form of maiming. This emphasis on maiming repeats the death anxiety of the earlier novel in the form of castration anxiety.[6] Both castration anxiety and death anxiety are closely related to Traven's precarious sense of identity. Significantly, the victims of most of the maimings and tortures described are the Ladino owners and overseers who have deprived the Indians of their identity and manhood.

According to the Professor, Martín Trinidad, the rebellion must destroy the Ladino's power to deprive the Indians of their identity. He urges the Indians to burn the documents which the Ladinos have used to take away their property and liberty. When the Indians leave the camp to return to their land they attack the small Spanish towns along the way. Trinidad urges them to

> attack the registry and burn the papers, all the papers with seals and signatures—deeds, birth and death and marriage certificates, tax records, everything. . . . Then the heirs won't ever come and stick their papers under our noses. Then nobody will know who he is, what he's called, who was his father, and what his father had. We'll be the only heirs because nobody will be able to prove the contrary. What do we want with birth certificates? We live with a woman we love, we give her our children. That's being married. Do we need papers to prove it? (P. 308)

The character of the Professor is a transparent disguise for the author, who has neither birth certificate nor legal father.

The Ladinos are disguised father figures. Like Gales-Traven's father, they made the Indians into illegitimate orphans. Rebellion symbolically castrates these father figures; they are deprived of their manhood in return for having deprived the Indians of theirs. Traven has his vicarious revenge on his father and on society for forcing anonymity upon him. When the documents are destroyed the Indians will be protected by their anonymity: "Then nobody will know who he is, what he's called" (p. 308). The Indians can triumphantly proclaim, like Gales of *The Death Ship:* "until the trumpets of the Last Day are calling . . . [men] will be confused as to how to call me."[7] Gales-Traven survived the wreck of the death ships to have his revenge in the unlikely setting of the jungle lumber camps. The Ladinos also suffer the dreaded anonymous death; the foremen and overseers are killed in the attack on the camp headquarters and their bodies are devoured by pigs.[8]

Don Felix in particular seems to represent the father-betrayer. His brutality results in the drowning of Candido's son and he compounds the crime by attempting to rape Candido's sister Modesta. Don Felix is responsible for the boy's dying without having his identity restored. The body is not reunited with the mother as in *The Bridge in the Jungle*; the mother figure, Modesta, is almost raped. The castration anxiety evident in the work is connected with the permanent separation of the child from the mother. Castration resembles the original separation at birth.[9] Throughout *The Rebellion of the Hanged* Traven attempts to dispel his fear of castration by externalizing it and directing it against the father figures.

Traven may have felt that *March to the Montería*, the novel immediately preceding *The Rebellion of the Hanged*, was the more successful of the two because it concentrates on Celso's revenge. Yet this book, like most of the others in the series, presents the central theme of betrayal and revenge in an externalized and weakened form. The novel is ostensibly concerned with the march of Celso and Andrés to the lumber camp where the rebellion is to take place, but Traven seems to be more interested in describing the murder of the two capataces [henchmen]. Celso had spent two years in a montería earning the money he needed to marry an Indian girl. But as a skilled mahogany cutter he is valuable to Don Gabriel, the labor contractor. Don Gabriel's two henchmen trick Celso into fighting with them, after which a corrupt judge sentences him to a long prison term. Since he cannot pay the exorbitant fine, the only way he can avoid jail is to contract himself for another two-year term in the montería in return for which Don Gabriel pays his fine.

Traven explains that the Indians cannot understand the system responsible for their plight, because it is too abstract. Celso focuses his anger on the two mestizo capataces who wronged him. On the long march to the montería, he plots his revenge. He fears nothing, for he is a man without a future: "From now on he would no longer care about anything. He would forget the girl, forget her father, forget his fifteen children. He belonged to the dead and so was free to do as he pleased."[10] Traven gives this rather trite analysis of the social system: Celso has been betrayed and deprived of his identity by the system that values profits over human lives. An Indian is worth only his strength and skill at cutting mahogany. Even Don Gabriel, who has to support a wife and family and has grown up in a system which considers the Indian to be merely a form of higher animal, is not ultimately responsible. Don Gabriel and the capataces are only instruments of the system.

On the long march Celso kills the first capataz, El Zorro, by clubbing him with a heavy branch, and placing his foot in the stirrup of his horse so that, goaded by the spur, El Zorro's own horse drags him to his death. "El Zorro's clothing was torn completely in rags, as thoroughly torn and ragged as his face. The head was a dirty pulp. There was hardly any flesh left on the skull and only a few tufts of hair. His neck was like a wash rag" (p. 182). The capataz is rendered faceless and nearly unrecognizable—an act reminiscent of Dobbs's beheading. Loss of identity and unmourned death are the prices paid by the capataz for participating in the betrayal of Celso.

Despite the parallels with *The Treasure of the Sierra Madre*, the psychological potential of the situation is not as well developed. Traven does not look into Celso's mind and reveal what he feels as he is committing the horrible deed. Although Traven's compulsive themes are present in *March to the Montería*, they are presented externally, as part of the adventure narrative. Traven is detached and takes obvious relish in Celso's bloody revenge, describing it with none of the terror or the paranoia that characterizes his best works. Because Celso is beyond fear, we cannot identify with him; neither can we identify with his victim, a brutal foreman who richly deserves his fate.

El Zorro's death is treated comically in a mock funeral sermon by the labor agent, Don Ramón:

> "Caballeros, it's God's eternal truth, he most certainly was a god-damned son-of-a-bitch, a filthy raper of innocent women, a scoundrel of a cattle rustler, a lousy pimp, a reptile, a venomous snake in the grass, a dirty bandit, a pitiless murderer and only God in Heaven knows what else, but after all, he was a human being and a Christian. And even if he's bound for hell, let's say an Ave Maria for his soul." (P. 187)

Traven can treat death in this comic fashion because he identifies with neither killer nor victim.

El Camarón, the other capataz who has helped to entrap Celso, is impaled on a stake. He is not even given a funeral sermon, but Don Ramón says that "judging from the way he stares at us, I would swear that by this time he's already cooking in hell. Anyway, I'm feeling kind of lousy around my belly" (p. 212).

The novel is interspersed with paeans to nature. Celso, given a choice between going to jail for six months and working off his fine in a montería for another two years, chooses the latter. He prefers life in the open jungle, as difficult as survival there might be. After the murder of the two capataces the Indians march on to the region where the caoba or mahogany grows. Celso points it out to Andrés in ecstatic terms: "Look around I say again. Here it begins, the vast savage land of caoba. . . . And believe you me, now that I'm back here once more, smelling caoba, I honestly think that I really couldn't live anywhere else. I almost believe that I was truly homesick for caoba" (p. 222). The novel ends with a lovely nature description: "Rose-colored birds were circling inquisitively over the camp. Perceiving no danger, they spiraled in wide arcs toward the sandy banks of the majestic river, finally glided down, walked leisurely on their long, thin legs as if on stilts into the slowly flowing water and began, rather solemnly, to fish" (p. 227). The beauties of nature appeal to Traven because they represent a world free of strife and exploitation. He views the Indians' ancient culture as one in which people lived in harmony with nature. The Spaniards have imposed their unnatural European culture on Mexico and the Indians' rebellion is an attempt to reestablish the natural way of life.

But when the Indians have murdered the Montellano brothers and their foremen, and have burned the documents, it is not certain that they will be able to return to their homes and live out their lives in their ancient and natural fashion. The final novel in the series, *The General from the Jungle* (1939), seems to suggest that they will not. This book is an exciting potboiler, filled with descriptions of battles between Indians and Ladino troops. The Indians capture fincas and small villages. At the end of the novel they found a village they call "Solipaz," [sun and peace]. An itinerant schoolteacher who strays into their camp tells them that Diaz had fled some sixteen months before, when they left the monterías. The Indians remain unsure of the political situation; government troops, federal police, and bandits roam the countryside, and the Indians must still fight to preserve their newly-won freedom. The book ends with their cry "Tierra y Libertad" [Land and Liberty], but the ending is ambiguous. Will they be able to keep their land and their liberty?

Two other novels in the series, *The Carreta* [*The Ox Cart*], and *The Troza* [*The Mahogany Trunk*] (1936), do not merit extended discussion. *The Carreta* is partly a travel guide to Chiapas province, and partly Traven's commentary on the system that trapped Andrés Ugalde first into the life of a carretero, and then into the life of a laborer in the monterías. He later appears as one of the leaders of the "rebellion of the hanged." *The Troza* deals with the expropriation of the monterías by the brutal Montellano brothers, and is filled with naturalistic details of life in the lumber camps. It provides a clear picture of the social conditions of prerevolutionary Mexico, but it lacks literary distinction.

The one novel that succeeds on its own, independent of the series, is the second, *Government*. *Government* is a novel without a hero, and the only one in the series without an Indian protagonist.

The "art of government" under the Diaz regime is represented by the figure of Don Gabriel Ordúnez, who becomes secretary of an Indian village. He proceeds from petty graft-taking to slave-trading when, later in the novel, he becomes a recruiting agent for the monterías. He appears in the later novels as the agent who recruits Andrés, Candido, and Celso for the montería that erupts in revolt. In this novel there is another, more limited revolt: the insistence of the independent Indian village of Pebvil on changing its leader once a year, against the will of the federal government.

Don Gabriel is an anti-hero, part of the system that exploits the Indians. But Traven does not condemn him, for he too is an underdog. His predicament is similar to Dobbs's: "So don Gabriel accepted the post [of village secretary]. He would have accepted the post of watching boiling cauldrons in hell if anyone had offered it to him. He was so down on his luck that he had no choice. It was getting on to twenty years since he had sought a way out in honest work." Don Gabriel "had a good revolver and he could shoot as straight as the next man,"[11] so he does not fear taking the job. Since the salary is not enough to support his family, he accepts the graft and the excessive taxes levied on the Indians as part of the system:

> No one expected a governor, a chief of police, a mayor, or a tax collector to live on his pay; nor did the jefe político imagine for a moment that he had to live on his.
>
> So it was also a matter for the secretary to consider how he was to arrive at a decent income for himself. The jefe político expected a good share of it, just as the chief of police looked to the police under his command for a share of their pickings, in order to feel justified in continuing to employ them. How they came by their pickings was no affair of his. They were all born with heads on their shoulders, and he had given them each a good revolver and invested them with ample authority. (P. 7)

The comic tone prevents the reader from identifying with Don Gabriel, and at the same time from identifying with the Indians and condemning Don Gabriel's treatment of them. Traven creates a distancing effect which works perfectly for the satire on the government, and at the same time keeps the irony from becoming too heavy-handed.

Later in the novel an acquaintance of Don Gabriel, a former cattle trader who has become a labor agent, persuades him to enter the more lucrative business: "I deal in other cattle. I am an agent for the monterías" (p. 120). The business is always "fine," for "a third, in some of the monterías, half, of the peons are dead within the year and have to be replaced; so business is never slack. It's a hundred times better than dealing in cattle and pigs or horses and mules" (p. 120). The irony is unsubtle, but Traven is making the point that the Ladinos as well as the Indians have been brutalized by the system. Don Gabriel believes that his change of profession is an act of self-sacrificing patriotism: "To deal in cattle was mere self-seeking. To recruit Indian labor in order to put production on a competitive level was, on the other hand, a patriotic activity" (p. 129). This dehumanized, exploitative Ladino culture clashes with the ancient democratic culture of the Indians of Pebvil.

Don Gabriel arrives in Pebvil just before the selection of a new cacique [leader]. On New Year's Day, the people of four federated tribes arrive at the square to watch the inauguration ceremony. The new chieftain sits on a chair with a hole in the middle under which is placed a pot filled with glowing charcoal.

> The fire under the chief's posterior was to remind him that he was not sitting on this seat to rest himself but to work for his people; he was to look alive even though he sat on the chair of office. Furthermore, he was not to forget who put the fire under him . . . and that it was done to remind him from the outset that he could not cling to the office but had to give it up as soon as his time was up, so as to prevent any risk of a lifelong rule. . . . If he tried to cling to his office they would put a fire under him that would be large enough to consume him and his chair. (PP. 175–76)

The new cacique must prove himself by listening to long speeches without moving, and even by making jokes about his situation: "There is no warmth at all coming up through the hole. Here you,

Eliseo, come here and scrape off the ice that is forming on my buttocks" (p. 176). This initiation and mock sacrifice of the ruler are brilliant satiric inventions.

The Indian political system conflicts with the decree of the Diaz dictatorship, which says that the present chief of the Indians has to remain in office:

> As Don Porfirio [Diaz] intended to sit there for life, and as the governor, too, hoped to be a lifelong governor, the governor declared the system in vogue at Pebvil a stupidity and a proof that nothing good could be expected of Indians, who were still sunk in barbarism. He commanded by decree that the present jefe, Amalio, had either to be elected again, or else to remain in office by virtue of the last election. (P. 183)

This present cacique, Amalio, had been accepting bribes from the local secretary; thus the Indian system is proved correct in providing a means of removing corrupt politicians from office.

Despite the governor's decree, the entire Indian nation, thousands strong, gathers in the square in front of the cabildo [town hall] for another inauguration. But Amalio refuses to give up the staff of office. If he did he would be guilty of treason to the federal government. The Indians' representatives deliver an ultimatum, and when the time is up some young men spring forward from the assembled crowd.

> Half like fleeing deer, half like charging tigers, they rushed precipitately around the edge of the crowd to the cabildo. It was hardly running—they sprang forward in long leaping strides, their bodies almost parallel with the ground. Each had a machete in his hand, and as he ran he held it outstretched in front of him. . . . A piercing cry tore into the silence that rested on the waiting crowd below. It came from Amalio's wife and it was the only sound that reached the square. The group around the new chief, who were closest to the cabildo, heard also a brief scuffle and the dull thud of falling bodies. (PP. 208–9)

The staff of office is thrown to the new chief:

> And now there came flying out of the schoolroom and over the balcony railing onto the grass below, first Amalio's head and then the heads

91

of his wife and children. Immediately after the heads came the bodies, hacked to pieces. (P. 209)

Traven's compulsive themes reappear in a new guise. When the cacique decides to remain in office he violates the ancient rules of his people, setting himself apart from them. He is a lackey of the Ladinos. For this betrayal, he suffers both the beheading experienced by Dobbs and the dismemberment feared by Gales in a horrible death symbolizing the loss of self. The inaugural scene ends as the crowd departs, knowing that their system has been preserved. The new cacique waves the staff of office, and they utter a "cry of triumph" that "was their parting act as one united people" (p. 210).

Although the anonymous Indians of Pebvil have triumphed in this matter, the system that threatened them remains intact. The book ends with Don Gabriel becoming rich as a labor contractor. Fourteen innocent Indians who are returning to Pebvil from a market are charged with the murder of Amalio and fined in lieu of a jail sentence. Don Gabriel pays their fines, distributes the necessary graft, and has a handsome profit waiting for him when the Indians reach the monterías to work off their debts. Under this political system the wicked prosper.

Government is a simple statement of anarchist antipolitics.[12] Its political theme is summarized by an Indian chieftain who is thankful for the departure of the last representative of the federal government: "I should like it best if the government forgot us for good. I have said all I have to say, my brothers and friends" (p. 167). Traven, in his article on *Government*, echoes the Indian chieftain: "Government is thoroughly, is always, oppression of some part of a people for the benefit of another part of these same people. What men need is organization and administration. What men do not need and what therefore must be done away with, is government."[13] This anarchist novel functions as a wish-fulfilling fantasy for an author who repeatedly depicts society as guilty of betrayal. It is only the anonymous Indians of Pebvil, with their ancient tribal traditions, who can escape the greed and irrationality of modern government.

Traven probably realized that *Government* is the best novel in the series, since it alone of the series is the subject of one of his essays. The author claims that his novel is a realistic representation of his "Indian brothers," and predicts that the Indian himself will eventually see that *Government* represents a greater honor to him than the works of the "fairy tale writer Cooper." In reading Traven's book the Indian will recognize his kinship with the European proletariat, and this brotherhood will be considered a "greater honor than the . . . honor from fairy tale books in which he is the brother and blood friend of the great warrior and chieftain 'Tiger Paw' of the noble tribe of the Delawares."[14] Although Traven claims to despise Cooper, it is probable that he was influenced by him. *The Death Ship* contains similar but more veiled attacks on Conrad and O'Neill. Traven seems to have regarded his literary influences as threatening father figures, and he is always hostile to them.

Traven gives us the following information about the early years of Stanislav, one of the characters in *The Death Ship*: "A couple of hundred stories in imitation of Cooper's *Last of the Mohicans*, sold at a dime apiece, and another couple of hundred sea-stories and pirate yarns, had ambushed his spirit, and he ran away from home."[15] Traven may have originally been attracted to the Indians and drawn away from Europe by similar readings. His flight from European society led him to the tramp ships, and then to Mexico, where life among the Indians afforded him an escape from the unanswerable questions about his identity. In the jungles of Chiapas he lived out the escape from civilization that he found depicted in Cooper's works:

> The author of the books [the Jungle Novels] has, with only short interruptions, spent more than two years in that region, without the company of men of his race. He has lived, danced, sung, travelled with Indians, mule-drivers, carreteros . . . attended Indian weddings, arranged Indian marriages and, with or without moonshine, sat and also not merely sat with young Indian maidens under trees. It was a cutting off of self from civilization.[16]

The experience produced *Government*, a novel that resembles Cooper's escape fantasy. And two years in the jungle "without the company of men of his race" relieved Traven of the need to lie about his identity. He lacked documents to prove it, but so did the Indians.

In *Government* Traven shows that the anonymity of the Indians is a successful defense against every threat of betrayal. The young Indians who kill Amalio and his family spring forward from the crowd:

> They clung so closely together as they ran that no one in the crowd could recognize their faces. Their movements, too, were so rapid and spasmodic that their faces were distorted. Their mouths gaped wide and their eyes were compressed to tiny slits. Their foreheads were furrowed deeply by their excitement and their long black hair floated about their heads. All this so disguised them that little was to be seen of their usual appearance. (P. 208)

Protected by their anonymity from reprisal, they quickly hack Amalio and his family to pieces with machetes, "and before any eye could hold them they had vanished into the bush on the far side of the square" (p. 210). Unlike Amalio, whose death represents a complete loss of self, the Indian avengers "disappear" only to merge with their land and people.

Traven hoped that his own anonymity would afford him complete protection from any further betrayal. But because his defense often seemed to crumble, as on the film set of *The Treasure of the Sierra Madre*, Traven created this wish-fulfilling fantasy in which anonymity affords complete protection to the avengers of Pebvil. Traven realized, however, that this success was an isolated one, that government is everywhere, asking for proof of identity, for documents. The story of this successful revolt is overshadowed by the story of the success of the rogue, Don Gabriel.

Government is a comic masterpiece which echoes the first book of *The Death Ship*. The bureaucratic society is moved to Mexico; expressionism with comic overtones is replaced by comic fantasy. The later novel is a satire on government in which all the laws are for the benefit of the Ladinos and to the detriment of the Indians. To Don Gabriel, the laws that allow him to profit are orderly and intelligible. To the Indians they are incomprehensible.

Traven's novel breaks all the accepted canons of novel writing: there is no focus on a central character, no sustained narrative line. It is a book without a protagonist, since Don Gabriel, far from determining the action, is only an agent of the system. The Indians here, unlike the protagonists of the other novels in the series, are anonymous; the people of Pebvil are the heroes. It is perhaps the absence of a sympathetic central character that creates the comic lack of affect which enables this book to succeed where the others in the series of Jungle Novels fail. In the other novels, Traven is outraged at the treatment of Andrés, Candido, Celso, and the other Indians uprooted from land and family. Yet he does not seem to feel close enough to his Indian protagonists to project himself and the reader into their psyches. When they have their revenge, the bloodshed and brutality become the focus of his interest. Without a character through whose mind the experiences can be filtered, that is, without a Gales or a Dobbs representing Traven himself, the brutal action fails to become psychological terror. Traven succeeds as a writer when the central character is his persona, as in *The Death Ship*; when that character represents some aspect of his personality, as in *The Treasure of the Sierra Madre*; or when, on the other hand, he is writing a comic fantasy in which there is no question of identification with the characters.

In his article on *Government*, Traven claims that his visits to the Mexican jungle were made to gather data for "documents." These documents were given the "form of novels for easier reading," and became the Jungle Novels.[17] The entire series is a naturalistic representation of the plight of the Mexican Indians before the revolution of 1910 in which Pancho Villa, Emiliano Zapata, Francisco Madero, and others overthrew the Diaz dictatorship.[18] A rebellion of mahogany workers actually did break out in the monterías of the Rio Usumacinta region where "Engineer Torsvan" traveled to gather information.[19] Danish explorers who went to the region in 1953 report that the "montería Romano," the model for the one owned by the Montellano brothers in the Jungle series, had been completely destroyed: "We arrived at the lake in the vicinity of which was located, before the revolution, the large houses and groves of the infamous Romano Co. Today there remains only stubble."[20] The Jungle Novels add a footnote to the historical documentation of a revolution dominated by the figures of Villa, Zapata, and Madero. But for these novels, the Indians' struggle for independence might have been forgotten.

It is largely because of the Jungle Novels that Traven is regarded in Mexico as an "authentic Mexican novelist."[21] Manuel Pedro Gonzalez, in his *Trayectoria de la Novela en Mexico* [*History of the Novel in Mexico*], says that Traven, in his depiction of the Indians, has "dramatized an important aspect of Mexican social reality."[22] National origin is not important, according to Gonzalez, in determining whether a writer should be regarded as belonging to Mexican literature. Only Traven has "penetrated into the idiosyncracies of the Indian, into his soul tortured by pain, hunger, and the maltreatment that Christian white men and mestizos have inflicted upon them for centuries."[23] Traven himself told Luis Suarez: "I am Mexican, born in the United States."[24]

Although the Jungle Novels in general may be regarded as a contribution to the history of the Mexican Revolution, *Government* is in no sense a factual presentation of the revolution. Traven's reading of Cooper and his fantasy of anonymity resulted in a fairy tale for adults who wish to escape from the encroachment of government. The ambiguous ending of the novel shows that Traven knew that escape was impossible—except for the anonymous Indians of Pebvil. *Government* is a wish-fulfilling fantasy in which reader and author can share with the Indians the satisfaction of compelling government simply to leave them alone.

6

The
Short
Stories:
"Godfather Death"

The short story "The Night Visitor" and the short novel "Macario" are among Traven's finest works. "The Night Visitor" and another short story, "Effective Medicine," were published in 1928, a year after *The Treasure of the Sierra Madre*. A third short story, "Midnight Call," was published in 1930. "Macario," Traven's last major work, did not appear until twenty years later.[1] In all of the short stories Gales reappears as Traven's protagonist, acting as doctor-medicine man to the Indians, and, like Howard at the end of *The Treasure of the Sierra Madre*, gaining a reputation for his miraculous cures. The protagonist of "Macario," a character of the same name, becomes a doctor in partnership with his "compadre" Death.

In "The Night Visitor" Gales is living alone, deep in the Mexican bush. He reads about Aztecs, Toltecs, and other Pre-Columbian civilizations in books from his neighbor's library, and then he has a "night visitor," an Aztec prince whose burial mound has been disturbed by pigs. Gales finds the mound and also the mummy of the Aztec prince. When he takes the mummy's jewelry, the Aztec visits him again, asking for the return of the gold ornaments. The neighbor, a doctor whose house Gales has been watching, returns, and Gales leaves the bush to escape from the strange visits. No natural explanation for the events is given, nor is a supernatural one suggested. John Wain remarks that the story is a "ghost story of the straightforward, unashamed sort," notable for the author's "complete imaginative identification with ancient Mexican beliefs about the soul."[2] But more important is Gales-Traven's identification with the Aztec prince.

The Aztec, even in death, suffers from Gales-Traven's compulsive fear of physical disappearance. Hogs have opened his burial mound and begun gnawing his calf with their snouts. He shows Gales the evidence on his first visit: "About six inches above the ankle there was a repulsive wound. 'This,' he explained, 'has been done by the hogs.' "[3] Hogs also devour the bodies of the Ladino oppressors in *The Rebellion of the Hanged*. But the significant difference is that in this case Gales has the power to save his alter ego by repairing the mound and keeping the hogs away. The Aztec comes to request Gales's help: "But you see, I am unable to defend myself. I am so utterly helpless and powerless. I am very much in need of a friend alive" (p. 28). Gales, the defenseless victim of *The Death Ship* and the fearful explorer of *The Bridge in the Jungle*, becomes the "friend alive" who has the power of reaching into the tomb. Here the descent is made willingly, unlike the forced descent of *The Death Ship*.

Gales's newly acquired power over death is closely connected with the theme of becoming a doctor which runs through the short stories and culminates in "Macario." Gales thinks that the Aztec at first mistakes him for the doctor: "At last I knew what he had come for. He believed me to be the doctor" (p. 27). Gales tries to grasp the Aztec's ankle to cleanse the wound, but he finds himself grasping only air. Since he cannot cleanse the wound, he goes to repair the funeral mound.

When Gales breaks into the mound he finds that he must inspect its contents:

My first intention was to leave the mound exactly as I had found it, save that I would close the hole I had broken in. Yet now, after having been inside and seeing its ghastly contents, I had no choice. No longer could I afford to leave everything inside as I had seen it. It would haunt me for the next twenty years. It might disturb the quiet of my mind forever. Most surely it would keep me awake for hundreds of nights and bring me to the verge of insanity. I would now be afraid to go into a dark room or sleep with all the lights out. (P. 32)

On the level of a ghost story the question is merely whether the mummy is the same person as the night visitor. But Gales's language recalls the unanswered questions about his identity that plague him in *The Death Ship*, questions that again appear in connection with descent into the womb which appears here as the tomb.

Gales does indeed find the mummy to be that of his night visitor, a mummy that "looked exactly as though the man had died only the day before yesterday, if not last night when I had seen him go to this mound" (p. 33). The body that Gales finds in the darkness of the tomb is in fetal position as is the body of little Carlos in *The Bridge in the Jungle:* "His elbows rested upon his knees. His head was bent down and his face was partly hidden in the palms of his hands. He sat as if in deep meditation or as if asleep" (p. 33). Gales as a "doctor" attempts to "deliver" the body of his double, but again finds himself grasping only air:

> I crept down into the cave with the intention of lifting the body up and getting it out of the cave. I grasped the body firmly, but I could not get a hold on it because my hands clapped together without anything between them save air.
> Between my grasping hands the body had collapsed entirely and nothing was left but a thin layer of dust and ashes which, if carefully gathered, would not have amounted to more than what a man might hold in his two hands. (P. 35)

Even after his mummy has crumbled to ashes,[4] the Aztec reappears to claim the jewelry that Gales has taken from the tomb. The bracelets, anklets, and necklace are gifts: "My nephew gave them to me when I had to leave him and all the others" (p. 27). Gales recalls reading that "after the death of the king not the son but the nephew of the king became the ruler of the people, a continuance which proved the Indians of old had a great knowledge of the natural laws of heredity of which we know so little" (p. 28). Thus the narrator-author who, as we know from the autobiographical

Death Ship, is an illegitimate outcast, attempts to show that there are alternatives to the conventional and supposedly natural father-to-son mode of inheritance.

After the ghost appears for the third and last time, Gales awakens and finds himself enveloped by a feeling of love: "There was about me a rich and wonderful feeling of true friendship and of immaterial love such as I could not remember ever having felt before, not even in the presence of my mother. I thought that if a similar state of feeling should accompany me when I was about to die, I would believe that there was nothing more wonderful than death" (p. 43). The Aztec prince serves as a father substitute, as we see in the previous passage on inheritance. But he also serves as a mother substitute, double compensation for Gales-Traven's orphandom. Parental love and the death compulsion are combined in the figure of the ghost.

The connection between love and identity is indicated by the Indian's explanation of the importance of the ornaments:

> "For love, and for nothing but love, is man born into this world. It is only for love that man lives. What else is the purpose of man on Earth?
>
> Therefore, my friend, pray return to me these little tokens [the gold ornaments] which you took away from me, misunderstanding their meaning. Return them to me tonight, because, after my long journey to the Great Gate, I shall need them. When I shall be questioned then, 'Where are your credentials, newcomer?' I must have them with me so that I may answer 'Behold here, oh, my Creator, here in my hands I carry my credentials. Few and small are these gifts, true, but that I was allowed to have them with me and wear them all along my way here—this is my evidence that I, too, was loved while on Earth, and so, my Lord and Maker, since I was loved, I cannot be entirely without worth.' " (P. 44)

The contrast between "The Night Visitor" and *The Treasure of the Sierra Madre,* written a year earlier, is sharp. As Judy Stone points out, "Those golden ornaments represented, not wealth, but the love felt for the prince by those who gave him the trinkets. The gold in

Treasure represents nothing but greed."[5] Unlike Dobbs, Gales returns the gold that he has taken. When he awakes the next morning, he finds it gone. Was it all a dream? This question, which is on the ghost story level, is unimportant. What is important is that the Aztec prince has had his identity restored. In restoring the treasure to the Aztec, Gales, the illegitimate, disinherited son has enabled him to travel to Paradise.

Gales, at the end of "The Night Visitor," leaves his house in the bush in search of his own tokens of identity and love. His neighbor, the doctor, explains that he too would like to leave but cannot: "I'm bound here, damn it. I'm buried here, bone, soul, heart, flesh, everything. Only ashes it is that you see. All of me is buried here. Only the mind is still alive. . . . You see, the thing is that I'm buried here in more than just one way" (pp. 52–53). The doctor, like the Aztec prince, is buried in the bush, and only his ashes remain. He "has died long, long ago" (p. 53) in the incredible loneliness of the Mexican bush. If Gales had remained, he too might have turned to ashes. Gales appears in two other stories, also set in the Mexican wilderness, but on the outskirts of Indian villages. In these, Gales himself plays the role of doctor to the villager. It is as if the spirit of the "dead" doctor has been transferred to Gales.

In "Effective Medicine," a minor, comic story, the Indians think that Gales, the gringo living in their midst, is a "white medicine man." A peasant whose wife has just left him asks Gales to locate her, threatening him with a well-sharpened machete. He knows that Gales can find her, for

> all people in the village here have told me that you are a far-seer. They have told me that you have two little black tubes sewn together to make them appear like one. They say, because they know, that if you look through these tubes you can see any man or woman or dog or burro which might walk on that faraway hill yonder, and you can see an eagle perching on a high tree a hundred miles away. (P. 66)

Gales proves that he is indeed a far-seer when he tells the machete-wielding man that his wife was abducted to a village five hundred

101

miles away. The new element here, just suggested in "The Night Visitor," is the dangerous aspect of having a reputation as a doctor; this theme is continued in "Midnight Call."

In "Midnight Call" Gales is awakened in the middle of the night by a knock on the door of his hut. He is afraid he will be murdered if he opens the door.

> Now, if someone in the countryside in the Republic knocks on your door around midnight, experience, advice, good taste and manners demand that you keep quiet, that you don't answer and that you hold your breath as long as possible, because it might just so happen that at the very moment you open the door to see who is there . . . you have two or a dozen shots fired at you, and you withdraw safe and unharmed or filled with lead, alone or followed by some men who push you farther inside and not exactly in a friendly way. (P. 130)

After further consideration he concludes that

> if things have already gone so far that you hear a violent knocking on your door at night and the knocking gets more vehement every second, it will no longer be of any use to sweat from fear. Whatever is going to happen, whatever it may be, that has already been decided outside without consulting you and so you'd better save the cold sweat. (P. 131)

Gales's situation is similar to his situation in the first book of *The Death Ship*, but the lighter tone suggests that it is easier for him to face death when the problem of his identity is for the moment put aside. At least Gales has a substitute identity, his reputation as an unlicensed gringo doctor.

The midnight callers turn out to be three members of a bandit gang. They want "Doctor" Gales to treat the nephew of one of them who was wounded in a hold-up. After Gales treats the boy, the bandits, who think that he may report them to the authorities, consider killing him. They are dissuaded by the boy's aunt who is grateful for her nephew's recovery and intelligent enough to realize that Gales is not interested in the criminal aspects of the case. When Gales escapes this hazard his troubles are not over. The authorities are looking for the gringo who cures the bandits they are trying to catch. Gales manages to escape from the soldiers who are sent to the village to find him by pretending that he knows nothing about medicine; he tells the officer, "when I see blood I faint right away. It makes me awfully sick" (p. 153). As usual, he survives by lying about himself.

The illegitimate outcast of *The Death Ship* has made his way to Mexico where he lives by his wits, and has his revenge on society for its failure to recognize him by aiding its enemies, the bandits. Gales escapes from the authorities because he is unlicensed and unrecognized. A police chief laments that it is difficult to catch the bandit doctor because "we haven't got a picture of him" (p. 158). Traven hid his identity and refused to be photographed out of fear of imaginary threats, but for Gales, in this story, these precautions are actual survival techniques.

The doctor theme suggests that Gales has found a satisfactory role to play in Mexico. Like being a stoker on the *Yorikke*, acting as a bandit doctor gives him a sense of identity which compensates for society's failure to recognize him. The illegal role brings its own risks, for bandits have no mercy on doctors whose cures are unsuccessful: "No doubts puzzled my senses as to what would happen to me should I fail" (p. 143). But the greatest significance of the role is that it gives Gales-Traven some control over death.

Traven counteracts his own death anxiety by giving Gales this power. Playing the role of doctor seems to "represent a counter-phobic defense" for Gales-Traven, as it does for many doctors who have an unusually "strong fear of death." Of Traven too it may be said that "part of the psychological motivation of the physician is to cure himself and live forever: he wishes to be a scientist in order to gain mastery over life."[6] Even Gales's flippant tone does not conceal the importance of his new power: "An able-bodied doctor . . . can now and then, if lucky, prolong the expiring of a dying human for a good length of time" (p. 143). Gales can do at least as much: the badly-wounded young bandit is well enough to make his escape the next morning. At the end of the story, when the rumors of his medical prowess take on epic proportions, Gales, fearing that fame will be accompanied by discovery, makes an escape to Mexico City.

Traven's preoccupation with the doctor theme continued for twenty-two years. He himself played the role of doctor-medicine man to the Indians of Chiapas: "The author . . . has helped bring little Indian babies into the world."[7] This role enabled him to put his fears to rest by participating directly in the process of birth and death. Playing the role of doctor unofficially and probably illegally, he did not report births, injuries, or deaths to the authorities and thereby avoided the documents he abhorred. "Macario," in which a Mexican protagonist plays the role of doctor, is the culmination of the doctor theme, and reveals the full significance of the theme for Traven.

"Macario" at first seems to be a simple folk tale. Macario, a poor Mexican woodchopper with eleven hungry children and a wife to support, shares his roast turkey with Death. In payment for the dinner, Death makes his new compadre, Macario, a doctor.

> I shall make you a doctor, a great doctor who will outwit all those haughty learned physicians and superspecialists who are always playing their nasty little tricks with the idea that they can put one over on me. That's what I am going to do: make you a doctor. And I promise you that your roast turkey shall be paid for a millionfold. (PP. 210–11)

Having a whole turkey to himself out of sight of his ever-hungry brood is the fulfillment of Macario's lifelong dream. Macario had refused to share his turkey with the Devil, or with Christ, who had both appeared before him. But when Death appears before him as the "Bone Man," he knows he cannot escape his destiny, and so shares his meal with Him. As Macario explains, "as long as he eats too, I will be able to eat, and so I make it fifty-fifty" (p. 210).

Macario and his new compadre, Death, share the turkey and feel "as jolly as old friends meeting each other after a long separation" (p. 207). This separation may be the twenty-four year time span between *The Death Ship* and "Macario," although the obsession with death is displayed to a lesser degree in all of Traven's works.

It may be a much older separation, dating back to Traven's childhood when he first felt the lack of a father. This feast may be compared with the ancient totem meal, but here it is the reconciliation with the father, rather than his murder, that is being commemorated.[8] In this communion Macario identifies himself with the father figure Death by sharing his meal with him. For his generosity, he obtains not "sanctity" but the power of a "great doctor." He specifically rejects the "sons," the Devil and Christ, as having no right to share in his feast. Macario and Death are thus each other's compadres, and Traven, vicariously, is at last "with father."

Perhaps there is an element of atonement here, as in the Christian rite. "Atonement with the father was all the more complete since the sacrifice was accompanied by a total renunciation of the women on whose account the rebellion against the father started."[9] Like the original rebellion of the sons postulated by Freud, the rebellion against the father in *The Rebellion of the Hanged* begins as a struggle over the possession of the mother figure. The attempted rape of Modesta sparks the violence which culminates in the overthrow and symbolic castration of the Ladino father figures. In "Macario," the work that represents atonement, the mother figure is absent. Death will give Macario his missing identity, so there is no need for a mother figure to receive her dead child. The descent and the death anxiety are replaced by a partnership with the father who is Death himself.

"Macario" contains Traven's final representation of death; death is personified as the protagonist's compadre and partner in his medical practice. Death gives him a bottle full of curing water, but tells Macario to use it only if "you see me standing at your patient's feet" (p. 213). But if, continues the Bone Man,

> "you see me standing at your patient's head, do not use the medicine; for if you see me standing thus, he will die no matter what you do and regardless of how many brilliant doctors attempt to snatch him away from me. In that case do not use the medicine I gave you because it will be wasted and be only a loss to you. You must realize, compadre, that this divine power to select the one that has to leave the

world—while some other, be he old or a scoundrel, shall continue on earth—this power of selection I cannot transfer to a human being who may err or become corrupt." (P. 213)

Macario gets not the power of selection, but only the power of curing those whom death has selected to be cured. He faithfully adheres to the agreement and becomes wealthy and famous.

When Macario is ready to retire, the Viceroy of New Spain asks him to cure his son. Macario is offered half the Viceroy's riches if he succeeds, but death at the hands of the Inquisition if he fails. He sees Death at the boy's head, and tries for the first time to cheat Death by turning the bed. "Macario, wild with madness, turned the bed around and round as if it were a wheel. Yet, whenever he stopped for taking a breath, he would see his dinner guest standing at the boy's head, and Macario would start his crazy game again by which he thought that he might cheat the claimant out of his chosen subject" (p. 233). But Macario recognizes that "his fate was upon him and that it would be useless to fight against it any longer" (p. 234).

Death does not save the Viceroy's son, but he does save his partner from being burned alive and grants him a painless death: "And this, compadre, I shall do for old friendship's sake, and because you have always played fair and never tried to cheat me. A royal payment you received and you honored it like a royal payment. You have lived a very great man. Good-by, compadre" (p. 234). Macario is saved from what seemed to be his fate because he did not betray his partner's trust. Death excuses Macario's attempt to save the boy because at the time his own life was in danger and he was "wild with madness." The beautiful fable ends with Macario's body being found in the woods by his wife and friends, with a half-eaten turkey in front of him and a "big, beautiful smile all over his face" (p. 234).[10]

Traven's story, which reads like a Mexican folk tale, is actually based on the Grimms' "Gevatter Tod" or "Godfather Death."[11] In using the folk tale as the basis for his short novel, Traven makes two significant changes. In the Grimms' story Death consents to become the godfather of a child whose father had befriended him. Since Death becomes Macario's compadre directly, Traven does away with the intermediate role of the father. Macario and his dinner guest are not godson and godfather but rather compadres. Death, which pursued Gales-Traven from Europe to Mexico, now becomes his best friend and surrogate father.

In Grimm the protagonist succeeds in cheating Death of two of his victims, for which Death gains his revenge at the end. The Grimms' Death, tricking his godson into thinking he will light a new candle of life for him, intentionally drops the old one. The tale ends with the ironic line: "At once the physician dropped to the ground and himself had fallen into the hands of Death."[12] Traven's Death, on the other hand, does his partner a favor when he grants him death. When Macario's wife finds her husband's body, she wonders who had been invited to eat the other half of the turkey; judging from the blissful smile on Macario's face, she thinks that "whoever he was, he must have been a fine and noble and very gentle person, or Macario wouldn't have died so very, very happy" (p. 235). Thus "Macario" presents the solution to the problem of betrayal: the protagonist, by not betraying his trust, gains the love of the all-powerful father figure.

"Macario" also presents the solution to the problem of Gales-Traven's death anxiety. Macario is both a doctor and a partner with Death. As a doctor he has some mastery over death and as Death's partner he can escape experiencing death as a punishment and can experience it as a reward. Macario accepts Death when he appears to share his meal and obeys his directives when they are partners. In doing so, he accepts his own death. In exchange for this acceptance he dies happily and peacefully.

From *The Death Ship* to "Macario," Traven's works display a fear of death and a pervasive anxiety which originates in this fear. They also reveal a deep-seated fear of betrayal, connected with paranoia and loss of identity. The relationship between these fears and the general anxiety may be elucidated by using Freud's idea of the stages of anxiety in the child's development. From a possible primal anxiety of birth, through castration anxiety to moral or social anxiety, the final stage of death anxiety is reached: "The final transformation which the fear of the super-ego undergoes is, it seems to me, the fear of death which is a fear of the super-ego projected on to the powers of destiny."[13] *The Death Ship* illustrates this final transformation, and "Macario" shows the fear allayed.

Gales's journey on the death ships results from the father's "betrayal," a betrayal disguised by being projected onto society. Society's bureaucrats, the substitute father figures, punish Gales by refusing to issue him an identity card, condemning him to the death ships. His descent into the stokehold gives him a substitute identity, but he must still be punished by the superego in the wreck of the *Empress*.

In "Macario" the father figure is merged with death itself in the figure of the Bone Man. Unlike Gales, who is forced to go on the death ships as a punishment for his illegitimacy, Macario himself chooses Death. Although he follows his source in this respect, it seems characteristic of Traven that his protagonist chooses as his compadre Death rather than Christ or the Devil.[14] Unlike his counterpart in Grimm, who chooses Death because he would make the most powerful godfather, Macario chooses Death because he knows that he cannot avoid his destiny. Death, the father, the superego, and the powers of destiny are all merged in Macario's new compadre with whom he feels "as jolly as old friends meeting each other after a long separation" (p. 207).

In Macario's reunion with Death, Traven depicts directly the final journey only hinted at for Stanislav and the Aztec prince. Gales only gazes in wonder at the apparitions of the death ship and his night visitor, but Macario makes the journey himself. The narrative has shifted from first to third person so that the author can separate himself from the protagonist and let him die. Traven disappears into his creation and his fears dissolve in Macario's blissful death.

Interestingly, the motif of descent into the underworld, present in the Grimm folktale, is absent in "Macario." In "Godfather

Death," after the godson cheated his godfather for the second time, Death seized him "with his icy hand so hard that he couldn't resist, and led him into an underground cavern."[15] This is the cavern where the candles of life are stored, and where the godson's life is soon to be snuffed out. In all of its appearances in Traven's works the motif of descent is accompanied by rebirth of a new identity. But in "Macario" the descent is not needed because the protagonist has an identity and a father. In death, which his compadre grants as a favor, Macario makes his final journey into a realm where not even the author may follow. Traven may be saying with Melville: "Our souls are like those orphans whose unwedded mothers die in bearing them: the secret of our paternity lies in their grave and we must there to learn it."[16]

"Macario" is Traven's final fantasy. The absent father, responsible for the anonymity and lack of identity of Gales-Traven, becomes compadre Death. The pervasive anxiety in Traven's work is transformed into Macario's beatific smile. Death is an after-dinner sleep, untroubled by the nightmare vision of the death ships.

Conclusion: B. Traven, Novelist and "Skipper"

The mystery of Traven's identity has focused attention on his life at the expense of his work. This is particularly true in America where, despite a growing underground reputation, his books have received little critical attention.[1] Perhaps scholars of American literature have felt uncomfortable dealing with a writer whose claim of being an American cannot be proven. Another obstacle may have been the language controversy surrounding the works. Since all of Traven's books first appeared in Germany, it seemed likely that they were written in German and then translated into English by someone else. The language problem, at least as far as *The Death Ship*, *The Treasure of the Sierra Madre*, and *The Bridge in the Jungle* are concerned, has now been resolved by Bernard Smith in an article in the *New York Times Book Review*. Smith, who edited these books for Knopf in the 1930s, says that he worked from English-language manuscripts supplied by Traven, but that these had to be heavily edited because they were filled with Germanic constructions. The manuscript of *The Death Ship* was "unpublishable, for it was the work of a man who was clearly ill at ease in English." Smith thinks that Traven "translated his own German into English literally, embellishing it occasionally with what he took to be American colloquialisms. Every other sentence was German in construction." Smith then undertook the rewriting of the books, while seeking to retain the "special flavor—the frequent awkwardness, the occasional stiltedness, the wavering union of toughness and sentimentality." He carefully adds that "there was nothing 'creative' about the work I did. I neither added nor subtracted. I inserted no thought or feeling of my own."[2] Unfortunately, such detailed information is not available about the English editions of the other works. These were probably edited by Traven's other literary collaborators, Esperanza Lopez Mateos and Rosa Elena Lujan, as well as by the publisher's editors. Whatever work may remain for textual scholars, Traven can now be considered as an American writer.

Traven's claim that he was born in America should be accepted as a fact, though an unverifiable one. However, he may not have spent more than a few childhood years in the United States, thereafter returning only for brief visits, as when he was married in San Antonio in 1957. Although his memorable protagonists, Gales, Dobbs, and Howard, are American, they too are expatriates, unable or unwilling to return home. After Howard chooses to remain with the Indians at the end of *The Treasure of the Sierra Madre* (1927), and Gales participates in the Indian funeral rites in *The Bridge in the Jungle* (1928), the protagonists in the works are Indian, beginning with *The Carreta* in 1931. So great was the lure of Mexican Indian life that from 1931 to 1940 Traven was solely engaged in writing the six Jungle Novels, his homage to the Indian "brothers of his heart."[3] In his last work of fiction, *Aslan Norval* (1960), Traven returns to the use of an American protagonist and, for the first time, places this protagonist in an American setting. The novel is an extravagant satire modeled after Twain's *The Gilded Age*. It concerns a woman, Aslan Norval, who has the desire to build a canal across the United States. The novel fails because Traven does not write believably about America and because the protagonist is vague and shadowy.

The main emphasis in this study has been on the psychological aspects of Traven's works, but it would also be possible to study them as social criticism, using a different approach and different primary sources.[4] *The Cotton-Pickers* (1926) could be used as an example of

111

Traven's possible affinities with the International Workers of the World.[5] In this novel, Gales is in Mexico working at odd jobs. Wherever he works, in cotton field, bakery, or restaurant, the exploited workers go on strike, apparently under the influence of Wobbly ideas; it seems likely that Gales, the American "outsider," is the source of these ideas. At the end of the book Gales is confronted by an American rancher for whom he has just driven a herd of cattle across the Isthmus. In answer to the ranch owner's accusation that he started the baker's strike, Gales claims it was "pure chance!—a strike always broke out where I was working or where I had been working, even if I'd hardly had time to look around me."[6] This autobiographical novel ends with Gales's characteristic refusal to reveal any information about himself.[7]

The most ambitious of Traven's works of social criticism is *La Rosa Blanca* (1929). A confrontation between Indian agrarian society and predatory American capitalism develops as the Indian Don Jacinto tries to protect his oil-rich hacienda, Rosa Blanca, from the Condor Oil Company. The oil company wins; Don Jacinto is murdered, deeds are forged, and the fertile land is desecrated by oil drills and derricks. The book suffers from simplistic social analysis, a mechanical plot, and, above all, from the wooden characterization of the American entrepreneur, Mr. Collins, who is a stock capitalist villain out of a 1930s proletarian novel. It is because of these flaws that Hill & Wang, the company currently engaged in publishing Traven's works, will not reprint this novel.[8] According to Luis Spota, "Croves" ranked Traven's works as follows: "*The Bridge in the Jungle* is the best of his books. *The Treasure of the Sierra Madre* is good. But *La Rosa Blanca* is detestable." He also added that *La Rosa Blanca* is "bad melodrama."[9] Traven himself should be allowed to have the last word about this novel and, by implication, about his merit as a writer of social criticism.

Traven agreed with one critic, Charles Miller, who found "Thoreauvian traits" in most of his books, "even in *The Treasure of the Sierra Madre*, with Howard's climactic disrespect for gold and his ability to live simply among his Indian friends; and even in the

112

bloody [*March to the Montería*], where the forced laborers learn to love the vibrant jungle and the tough mahogany trees to which they are enslaved."[10] "Croves" told Judy Stone that Miller "actually came near the meaning of Traven's books when he said that Traven's fundamental idea is like Thoreau's." He went on to say that *La Rosa Blanca* is not just a story of petroleum: "It is what the soil means to poor farmers. Don Jacinto picks up two handfuls of soil and looks at it and begins to cry as if to say that it is God Himself. God has personified Himself in that handful of soil. . . . This nearness to the soil is the most frequent and most important element in Traven's books."[11]

Throughout his life Traven thought of man's connection with nature in mystic terms. Señora Lujan says that at the time of his death "he was working on a theory that had preoccupied him since he was very young: a relationship [between man] and the sun."[12] This interest is reflected in *The Creation of the Sun and the Moon*, Traven's version of an Indian creation myth.[13] After the sun has been extinguished by evil gods Chicovaneg, a Tzeltal Indian chieftain, wanders through the sky collecting fragments of stars and placing them on his burning shield to create a new sun. Chicovaneg, who leaves his wife and son on earth to wander alone through the heavens, exiled himself voluntarily in order to save mankind. Thus he serves the human community even in his isolation. Traven seems to have wanted the world to view him as he portrays Chicovaneg in the myth: a creator standing in splendid isolation.

Traven's works bear some resemblance to those of the "hard-boiled" school of writing, which includes Dashiell Hammett and Raymond Chandler. Since some of Hammett's stories appeared in the pulp magazine *Black Mask* in the 1920s, they could have influenced Traven's writing of *The Treasure of the Sierra Madre* (1927),[14] for it was consciously written in the genre of pulp fiction. The following criteria have been suggested for determining whether a writer belongs to this school: his characters must exhibit "physical durability and maintenance of the stoic pose" and the "power to confront death without morbid pessimism."[15] Traven's characters have physical stamina, but the other more important criteria are not generally met. Gales and Dobbs are not stoic characters; and Gales, who suffers from fear of annihilation, fails to meet the third test. A distinction should be made between Traven's American protagonists and his Indian and Ladino characters. The Indians and Ladinos *are* stoic, but by nature, not as the result of a pose which, in the case of Hammett's and Chandler's characters, often serves to hide an underlying sentimentality. Traven's Indian and mestizo characters display a resignation to their fate; the Ladinos preserve their dignity to the last. Toward the end of *General from the Jungle* (1939), two Ladino officers are captured by the Indians. The lieutenant, about to be hanged, addresses his general:

> He drew himself up, stepped close to his commanding officer, looked him straight in the face, and said in clipped military tones, "Excuse me, sir. I wish to take indefinite leave. With your permission."
> Thereupon he saluted: "*Mi general, a sus ordenes!* Adiós, mi general!"
> The general held out his hand to him, drew him close, embraced him, let him go again, saluted likewise, and said, "*Adiós, muchacho! Adiós, Lieutenant Bailleres.* We will meet again in a few hours. Hasta la vista!"[16]

Although his deepest sympathies are with the Indian revolutionaries, Traven obviously admires the Ladinos' ability to face death not only fearlessly but with style.

Jack London is another writer of adventure novels who is often mentioned in connection with Traven.[17] Both are radical writers of adventure narratives; each used Mexican settings, each wrote of the search for gold, and each wrote a sea story that shows the influence of Melville. But Traven's *The Death Ship* and London's *The Sea Wolf* are modeled after *Moby-Dick* in very different ways. London's affinity with Melville is on the level of plot, subject matter, and characterization; Traven's is on a deeper psychic and symbolic level. Traven, like Melville, is concerned with the orphan and the exile, and their search for identity; London focuses on the all-powerful captain. This deeper dimension raises Traven above the category of adventure writer.

Traven never quite solved the problem of form. The structures of his best books are adaptations from other writers. *The Treasure of the Sierra Madre* is an updating of Chaucer's "The Pardoner's Tale" combined with an adventure narrative. "Macario" also has an archetypal motif; the Grimm tale "Godfather Death," which is its source, has many analogues in folklore and myth. *The Death Ship* borrows theme and structure from *Moby-Dick* and the *Inferno*. *Government* is the one completely successful work in which Traven relies on his own invention to supply the structure; but since *Government* is a short novel centering around one important incident, the revolt of the Indians of Pebvil, the problem of form is not crucial. The rest of the Jungle Novels fail largely because they lack the form that would act as a restraint on Traven's political digressions and gratuitous violence.

Traven wrote three excellent novels and several shorter works of the first rank; these should gain him recognition as an important writer. *The Treasure of the Sierre Madre* is probably his best work. The perfection of its symbolism allows it to succeed both as a study of paranoia and as a modern exemplum. *The Death Ship* is a powerful sea story which depicts the schizoid state of living death. The reviewer for the *Herald Tribune*, overwhelmed by the book, asked, "Has a new genius come out of the stokehold of some ocean tramp?"[18] And James Hanley, himself a writer of adventure narratives, said, "*The Death Ship* is the finest sea story I have ever read. . . . I can think of only one other book to stand beside it, and that an old one, *Two Years Before the Mast*.[19] For all its literary allusions, *The Death Ship* conveys a sense of immediacy which suggests that the author has just emerged from the stokehold to narrate his disguised autobiography. *Government*, another one of Traven's better works, strikes a new tone, that of comic fantasy. Like all of his works, it revolves around the deep-seated desire to escape, in this case from demands made by omnipresent government institutions.

Some of Traven's short works are also outstanding. John Wain, who reviewed *The Night Visitor and Other Stories* for *The New York Review of Books,* was inspired to comment: "However it comes, I feel sure that recognition for Traven is not far off, and when it comes it will be resounding. He is the only living writer who is capable of rivaling the Conrad of *Nostromo* and *The Shadow Line.*"[20]

Wain may have compared Traven with Conrad because, at their best, both create compelling narratives rich with symbolic meaning. Like Conrad in *The Nigger of the Narcissus,* and Melville in *Moby-Dick,* Traven is concerned with the individual's struggle against death. This struggle is the key to Traven's life and work.[21] As Gales says near the end of *The Death Ship:* "All we have is our breath. I shall fight for it with teeth and nails. I won't give up and I won't give in. Not yet. Not to the ground port."[22]

Traven had a life long obsession with the problem of identity. Spota reports: "Without anyone knowing exactly how, Traven got started on an emotion-producing topic . . . the identity of individuals."[23] Traven clearly wanted to believe that a person's sense of his own identity could suffice: "I do not need any papers; I know who I am."[24] But his refusal to reveal his real name shows that society's demand for documents and legal names had a profound effect on him. He developed the fantasy that he was in fact anonymous; that is, since "it had never been clear if [his] father had really added his name or not," he acted as if he did not have any real name. Because society equated names with identity, however, he gave himself three pseudonyms, all obviously coined.

These coined names enabled Traven to communicate with others while playing the roles of agent, "engineer," and writer. Adapting R. D. Laing's analysis of the "divided self," we can say that Traven "could either 'be himself' when he was anonymous or incognito, i.e. when he was not known to others, or he could let himself be known to others if he was not being himself."[25] Traven's pseudonyms seemed to insure that he could be "known to others" while "not being himself." In fact, he had a wide circle of friends among Mexico's intellectual community. They respected his need for an-

onymity and knew him as "Hal Croves," who supposedly wrote
books under the pseudonym of B. Traven.[26]

In 1969 a Norwegian journalist went to see Traven in his home
after being warned by Señora Lujan: "You now know he is Traven,
but do not forget that you want to see Hal."[27] His conversations
with Traven reveal a new development in Traven's concern with
identity—his attempt to live out the death ship fantasy. The reporter expressed his puzzlement to Traven's stepdaughter:

> "I do not want to ask any indiscreet questions, but why do you call
> your stepfather 'Skipper'?"
> She looks at me with big eyes and a sarcastic smile on her face,
> which is not flattering at all. It says that I am stupid.
> I now admit that it was a stupid question.
> "But *The Death Ship?*" she says.[28]

"B. Traven" did not exist even within the family circle. The inner
self could make itself known to others, but only as the "Skipper."
Traven's studio was "The Bridge," to which all but his wife were
forbidden entry.[29] Even though the ceiling of the studio was "badly
cracked from an earthquake . . . he refused to let workmen in to
make repairs."[30] Traven said, "Everything must be saved as if it
were a ship."[31]

Señora Lujan described home life with the "Skipper": "He was
the skipper on the bridge. I was the first officer, my older daughter
was the second officer, and my younger daughter the third. He'd
say, 'Second, do this, First, do that.' We'd say, 'Let's go below for
dinner.' Never downstairs, because that's bad luck."[32] Nothing
could be allowed to shatter the fantasy; Traven's life and works
were completely interfused. In the fantasy at the end of *The Death
Ship*, Gales had imagined himself master of the *Empress*. He had
also indirectly portrayed himself as captain of the *Yorikke:* "The
skipper was still a young man, hardly more than thirty-five. About
five seven in height. . . . His hair was brownish-yellow. . . . His eyes
were light waterish blue."[33] Traven was thirty-six years old when
The Death Ship was published and the physical description of the
skipper matches his own.

Traven's own experiences appeared in *The Death Ship*, and Gales's experiences were later reenacted by Traven. On the day after Traven's death, Señora Lujan told the Mexican press of her honeymoon: "We were married in the United States. The honeymoon was in New Orleans. From there Gales, the character of *The Death Ship*, embarked for Tampico. [Gales] is the character he identified with himself. . . . We also went to Antwerp, where Gales lost his ship."[34]

Traven's playing the role of "Skipper" can be seen as an attempt to prolong the voyage aboard the *Yorikke* indefinitely. On the *Yorikke* the question of identity was temporarily resolved. Traven becomes a skipper in his home to achieve absolute and permanent immunity from questions of identity.

As the "Skipper" of the ship, he is the "old man" or father to his crew of wife and stepchildren. The identity of skipper and father is demonstrated at the end of *The Death Ship* when Gales imagines that Stanislav is welcomed by God the father in the form of the "Great Skipper." Gales hallucinates a castaway's paradise: "And the Great Skipper said to him: 'Come, Stanislav Koslovski, give me your hand. . . . Never mind the papers. You will not need any.' "[35] Traven, in the sanctuary of his "Bridge," was living out the wish of being his own father, and neither death nor lack of identity could threaten him.

"Skipper" was also the role Traven created to communicate with those who were close to him, his family. The fantasy of being anonymous or incognito, carried to an extreme, leads to a psychotic condition in which one is "disconnected from all others and uncoupled even from a large part of one's own being." Traven understood that the "sense of identity requires the existence of another by whom one is known."[36] So he created the final role of Skipper. This role, which he played with his own family, kept him from being totally disconnected from others, while at the same time functioning as a defense against the exposure of the true, inner self.

In his life Traven avoided the total disappearance he feared by disappearing behind the mask of pseudonyms. The obsessive motif of descent into the womb, which appears in his works, is another form of controlled disappearance. The motif may be called "disappearance and return," which is the phrase Freud uses in his analysis of a child's game in *Beyond the Pleasure Principle*. A child made objects "disappear" by tossing them over the edge of a cot, and then retrieved them, with evident satisfaction, by means of an attached string. This game, which was to compensate for his having allowed his mother to go away without protesting, was followed by another in which the child made "himself disappear" by crouching below the level of a mirror.[37] Laing says that the latter game embodies a "schizoid presupposition by the help of the mirror, whereby there are two 'hims', one *there* and the other *here*."[38] Traven splits himself in two when he makes his alter ego Gales disappear into the womb of the death ship and then return. He also splits himself in two when he makes his alter egos Stanislav, Dobbs, Carlos, and the Aztec prince, his "mirror images," disappear forever. In a sense he is "killing himself in a magical way [by] killing the mirror image of himself."[39]

Traven was concerned that his body might disappear by being devoured. Luis Suarez reports that just before his death "He ordered that he not be buried, but rather that his body be cremated, as it was. 'I do not want to be eaten by worms,' he would say, accompanying the sentence with a gesture of putting his hands over his face, each day become ever-thinner."[40] Traven's fear of being devoured after death is related to his fear of being engulfed by others in life. Cremation prevented mutilation; destruction and "disappearance" of his body was within his own control. Gales's great fear is that if he were to drown "nothing would have remained for Judgment Day. . . . I would like to see how they settle this affair of collecting all the sailors out of a hundred thousand millions of fish bowels."[41] The Ladinos of the Jungle Novels are punished by having their bodies devoured. The Aztec prince of "The Night Visitor" seeks protection from the hogs who are gnawing at him. Dobbs, when he is beheaded, "disappears" after having lost himself to his paranoid fears. When Traven himself finally faced the threat of death, he could not send an alter ego on the journey of disappearance and return. He asked his wife to "scatter his ashes over various places: the waters of the Pacific Ocean, that inspired *The Death Ship*; Jackson Square in New Orleans, where the newlyweds spent their honeymoon; the anguish-filled jungle of Chiapas, that inspired [*The Bridge in the Jungle*] and *The Rebellion of the Hanged*; the Sierra Madre, in search of treasure."[42] These are the places crucial to Traven's fiction. Señora Lujan, in scattering the ashes, acts as the "friend alive" and performs a final, almost magical act of love comparable to Gales's returning the gold to the prince in "The Night Visitor." This act merges Traven with his work and heals the triple split in his personality.

Notes

Notes to Chapter 1

1. Luis Suarez, "Al Borde del Fin, Traven Pensó en un Escopetazo al Estilo Hemingway," *Siempre!*, 9 April 1969, p. 15.

2. This writer sent for Traven's birth certificate and received a "Certification that Record Was Not Found."

3. *The Cotton-Pickers* was serialized in the Berlin newspaper *Vörwarts* in 1925. It was published as a novel in 1926, a few months after *The Death Ship*.

4. "Mein Roman: *Das Totenschiff*," *Die Buchergilde*, no. 3 (1926): 34.

5. The first American publications of the major novels were as follows: *The Death Ship* (1934), *The Treasure of the Sierra Madre* (1935), and *The Bridge in the Jungle* (1938). For reviews of *The Death Ship* see John Chamberlain, *New York Times*, 18 May 1934, p. 21; Lincoln Colcord, "A Powerful Book, Unfettered, Wild," *The New York Herald Tribune Books*, 3 May 1934, p. 5; Mark Van Doren, "Men Without Countries," *The Nation*, 16 May 1934, p. 570. For reviews of *The Treasure of the Sierra Madre*, see Fred T. Marsh, "*The Treasure of the Sierra Madre* & Other Works of Fiction," *New York Times Book Review*, 9 June 1935, p. 6; Granville Hicks, "Proletarian Mystery," *New Masses*, 16 July 1935, p. 23; William Troy, "Radix Malorum," *The Nation*, 17 July 1935, p. 79. For a review of *The Bridge in the Jungle*, see Alfred Kazin, "*The Bridge in the Jungle* & Other Works of Fiction," *New York Times Book Review*, 24 July 1938, p. 6.

6. "On the Trail of B. Traven," *The Publisher's Weekly*, 9 July 1938, p. 106.

7. "B(ashful) Traven," 22 November 1970, p. 2.

8. Ibid.

9. The story of Traven and the filming of *The Treasure of the Sierra Madre*

121

Notes

is reported in Dwight Whitney, "More About Traven," *Life*, 2 February 1948; and *"The Treasure of the Sierra Madre," Time*, 2 February 1948.

10. Whitney, "More about Traven," p. 66.

11. Ibid.

12. "B. Traven Betrayed," *Life*, 15 March 1948, p. 23; "The B. Traven Mystery," *Time*, 15 March 1948, p. 13.

13. Luis Spota, *"Mañana* Descubre la Identidad de B Traven," *Mañana*, 7 August 1948, p. 14.

14. Spota, "la Identidad," pp. 17–18.

15. Ibid., pp. 22–25.

16. Ibid., pp. 24, 26.

17. Luis Suarez, *"Siempre!* Revela, al fin, El Misterio Literario Mas Apasionate del Siglo y Presenta al Mundo a B. Traven!," *Siempre!*, 19 October 1966, pp. 4, 6.

18. Suarez, "El Misterio Literario," pp. 8–9.

19. Judy Stone, "Conversations with B. Traven," *Ramparts*, October 1967, p. 57. Stone thinks that Traven was in fact the illegitimate son of Kaiser Wilhelm II, although she finds no direct evidence to support the theory. Her findings are reported in "The Mystery of B. Traven," *Ramparts*, September 1967. In Germany Traven is evidently thought to be the son of the Kaiser. See "Er ist ein Sohn des Kaisers," *Stern*, 13 April 1969.

20. Stone, "Conversations," p. 62.

21. Ibid., p. 59.

22. William [Weber] Johnson, "B. Traven: His Secrets & Passion for Anonymity," *Book Week*, 25 May 1969, p. 9; Suarez, "Al Borde del Fin," p. 15.

23. William Weber Johnson, "The Traven Case," *New York Times Book Review*, 17 April 1966, p. 42.

24. Rolf Recknagel, *B. Traven: Beiträge zur Biografie* (Leipzig: Reclam, 1971), pp. 225, 235, 423.

25. Johnson, "B. Traven: His Secrets," p. 9; Suarez, "Siempre: Desentraña, Al Fin, La Misteriosa Actividad de Traven en la Selva de Chiapas," *Siempre!*, 7 May 1969, pp. 34–36, 70.

26. Stone, "Conversations," p. 66.

27. Johnson, "B. Traven: His Secrets," p. 9. The German scholar Rolf Recknagel also believes Traven was Ret Marut. His findings were first published in his *B. Traven: Beiträge zur Biografie* (Leipzig: Reclam, [1966]); see also the later, more comprehensive edition (1971). Judy Stone summarizes his findings in "Mystery."

Notes

28. Recknagel, *Beiträge zur Biografie* (1971), p. 50.

29. Ibid., pp. 38–39.

30. Ibid., pp. 62–63, 109–10.

31. Ibid., p. 9.

32. *Khundar*, 1920, reprint ed., (Egnach, Switzerland: Clou Verlag, 1963), p. 72.

33. "Mein Roman *Das Totenschiff*," p. 37.

34. Enrique Loubet, Jr., "Falleció Ayer el Novelista, B. Traven," *Excelsior*, 27 March 1969, p. 35.

35. *The Death Ship, The Story of an American Sailor* (New York: Collier, 1962), pp. 53, 113.

36. "Conversations," p. 66–67.

37. "Mystery." The entire article deals with Ret Marut, his probable connections with B. Traven, and the possibility that Traven, alias Marut, was the son of the Kaiser. The article makes fascinating reading, but, as Stone herself realizes, there is no way of proving Marut's paternity or original nationality.

38. "Wer ist der Mann, der Traven heisst?," *Stern*, 7 May 1967, p. 172.

39. *Beiträge zur Biografie* (1971), p. 31.

40. "la Identidad," p. 21.

41. *The Death Ship*, pp. 55–56.

42. "Traven," "Torsvan," and "Croves" are not to be found in any genealogies or dictionaries of names for America, Germany, England, or Scandinavia. "Marut," a more obviously coined name, figures in Indo-Aryan and Teutonic mythology as a storm spirit. Jacob Grimm, *Teutonic Mythology* (New York: Dover, 1966) 4: 1471. Gales, the name of Traven's narrator, has a related meaning. The name "B. Traven" suggests the word "betrayed."

43. Spota, "la Identidad," pp. 22–23.

44. Johnson, "The Traven Case," p. 42.

45. *The Death Ship*, pp. 109–10.

46. *Moby-Dick* (New York: Hendricks House, 1962), p. 487.

47. *Herman Melville* (New York: Viking, 1957), p. 23.

48. *The Death Ship*, p. 187.

49. *The Divided Self* (New York: Pantheon, 1969), p. 138. Laing treats "ontological insecurity" in a chapter with that title, *The Divided Self*, pp. 40–64.

50. Whitney, "More About Traven," p. 24.

51. "Conversations," p. 66.

52. Mary Blume, "Clearing up the Mysteries of Author B. Traven," *Los Angeles Times*, 19 July 1970, p. 20.

53. *The Death Ship*, p. 118.

Notes to Chapter 2

1. Larry Doerflinger, "Hell Afloat," *Saturday Review of Literature*, 5 May 1934, p. 677.

2. *The Death Ship*, p. 28. Subsequent page number references in the text of this chapter are from this edition of *The Death Ship*.

3. "Mein Roman *Das Totenschiff*, p. 37. Traven does not state directly that the novel is autobiographical but his entire article suggests that this is the case. He does say that "whoever could write another conclusion has never been a solitary shipwreck who has just had his last comrade washed overboard."

4. Loubet, "Falleció Ayer el Novelista B. Traven," p. 35. Traven's widow is quoted as saying that "Gales, the character of *The Death Ship* . . . [was] the character [Traven] identified with himself." Furthermore, Traven himself, "years later, still had the scars of a stoker."

5. Professor Rolf Recknagel suggests the *Yorikke*-Yorick parallel in his *Beiträge zur Biografie* (1971), p. 144.

6. "Conversations," p. 65.

7. *Moby-Dick*, p. 318.

8. "Mein Roman *Das Totenschiff*," pp. 37, 38.

9. "Men Without Countries," p. 570.

10. "The Importance of B. Traven," *Chimera*, 4, no. 4 (1946): 46.

11. *The Great Tradition* (New York: Macmillan, 1935), p. 310.

12. "Mein Roman *Das Totenschiff*," p. 37.

13. "Conversations," p. 60.

14. It is interesting to note that James Hanley, comparing Traven to Conrad, states unequivocally that "*The Death Ship* is the finest modern sea story I have ever read." "Sugi-Mugi," *The Spectator*, 26 January 1934, p. 131.

15. "The Brute," *A Set of Six* (Garden City, N.Y.: Doubleday, 1924), p. 115.

16. Ibid., p. 112.

17. Ibid., p. 114.

18. Doerflinger, "Hell Afloat," p. 677.

19. *Moby-Dick*, p. 4.

20. The idea of a ship of death which is also a microcosm of society may be descended from Sebastian Brand's *Ship of Fools*, which Traven might have known through *The Confidence-Man*.

21. *Billy Budd, Sailor*, ed. Harrison Hayford and Merton M. Sealts, Jr. (Chicago: University of Chicago Press, Phoenix Books, 1962), p. 51.

22. Ibid., p. 52.

23. *Moby-Dick*, p. 420.

24. *The Inferno*, trans. John Ciardi (New York: New American Library, Mentor, 1954), p. 283.

25. "The Novels of B. Traven," *Horizon*, July 1940, pp. 523–24.

26. *Moby-Dick*, pp. 161–62.

27. *Moby-Dick*, p. 166.

28. Ibid.

29. *Jokes and Their Relation to the Unconscious* (New York: Norton, 1963), pp. 96–97.

30. Ibid., pp. 229–30.

31. The connection between Traven's insistence on anonymity, his fear of "vanishing," and his repeated theme of death by drowning is dealt with in chapter 4.

32. H. M. Tomlinson, "The Death Ships," *The Manchester Guardian Weekly*, 26 January 1934, p. 75.

33. Chamberlain, *New York Times*, 18 May 1934, p. 21.

Notes to Chapter 3

1. William Troy's review of the novel is entitled "Radix Malorum," *The Nation*, 17 July 1935, p. 79.

2. B. Traven, *The Treasure of the Sierra Madre* (New York: Hill & Wang, 1968), p. 1. Subsequent page number references in this chapter are to this edition of *The Treasure of the Sierra Madre*.

3. Charles H. Miller, for example, entitles a recent article "B. Traven, Pure Proletarian Writer," in *Proletarian Writers of the Thirties*, ed. David Madden (Carbondale: Southern Illinois University Press, 1968), pp. 114–33).

4. This projection illustrates the mechanism of paranoia formulated by Freud. "Psychoanalytic Notes Upon an Autobiographical Account of a Case of Paranoia (Dementia Paranoides) (1911)," *Three Case Histories* (New York: Collier, 1968).

5. The process is akin to that described by Freud in *Totem and Taboo* (New York: Norton, 1950).

6. Quoted by Professor Rolf Recknagel in a letter to me.

7. "Conversations," p. 65.

8. See, for example, Troy, "Radix Malorum"; T. A. Kirby, "The Pardoner's Tale and *The Treasure of the Sierra Madre*," *Modern Language Notes*, 66 (1951): 269–70.

9. This resolution of the novel recalls similar endings in D. H. Lawrence, particularly in *St. Mawr* and "The Woman Who Rode Away."

10. Marie Bonaparte, *The Life and Works of Edgar Allan Poe: A Psychoanalytic Interpretation* (London: Imago Publishing Co., 1949), p. 363.

11. Ibid., p. 366.

12. Ibid., p. 363.

13. Ibid., p. 365, 364.

14. "la Identidad," pp. 22–23.

15. This aspect of the book is singled out for special praise by Chamberlain, *New York Times*, 11 June 1935, p. 19, and Horace Gregory, "In the Mexican Mountains," *New York Herald Tribune Books*, 9 June 1935, p. 5.

16. See, for example, Henry Bamford Parkes, *A History of Mexico* (Boston: Houghton Mifflin, 1966), p. 385; J. Patrick McHenry, *A Short History of Mexico* (New York: Doubleday, 1962), p. 198.

17. The same historical situation is dealt with in Graham Greene's *The Power and the Glory*.

18. This point is stressed in the review by Marsh, "*The Treasure of the Sierra Madre* & Other Works of Fiction," p. 6.

19. "Proletarian Mystery," p. 23.

Notes to Chapter 4

1. B. Traven, *The Bridge in the Jungle* (New York: Hill & Wang, 1967), p. 8. Subsequent page number references in this chapter are to this edition.

2. Primitivism in the chapter title is used in the sense of the doctrine that primitive man, because he is closer to nature, is nobler than civilized man. Primitive life, treated from this point of view, is the ostensible subject of *The Bridge in the Jungle*. I attempt to show, however, that the emphasis in the novel is on Gales and his reaction to the death of the little boy rather than on primitivism itself.

3. "Traven über sein Buch 'Die Brücke im Dschungel,'" *Die Buchergilde*, no. 3 (1929), as quoted by Professor Rolf Recknagel in a letter to me.

4. Melville, p. 342.

5. "Traven über sein Buch 'Die Brücke im Dschungel.' "

6. B. Traven, letter to Manfred George, 1929, quoted by Professor Rolf Recknagel in a letter to me.

7. B. Traven über sein Buch 'Die Brücke im Dschungel.' "

8. The title character of *Aslan Norval* (1960) is an American woman with a "Scandinavian" name. This minor work is briefly discussed in chapter 7.

9. *The Death Ship*, p. 232.

10. Joseph C. Rheingold, *The Mother, Anxiety, and Death: The Catastrophic Death Complex* (Boston: Little, Brown & Co., 1967), p. 99.

11. Ibid.

12. *The Death Ship*, p. 118.

13. "la Identidad," p. 24.

14. *Moby-Dick*, p. 487.

15. "Traven über sein Buch 'Die Brücke im Dschungel.' "

16. Charles Miller, "B. Traven, American Author," in "B. Traven, A Special Section," ed. Charles Miller & R. E. Lujan, *Texas Quarterly* 6, no. 4 (1963): 165.

17. "*The Bridge in the Jungle*," p. 6.

18. "Traven über sein Buch 'Die Brücke im Dschungel.' "

Notes to Chapter 5

1. The six novels are *The Carreta* (1931), *Government* (1931), *March to the Montería* (1933), *The Troza* (1936), *The Rebellion of the Hanged* (1936), and *The General from the Jungle* (1939).

2. *The Rebellion of the Hanged* (New York: Knopf, 1952), p. 94.

3. Blinding, according to Freud, is symbolic castration.

4. Traven himself points out that he uses the "war cry of Zapata" in Stone, "Conversations," p. 65. The definitive work on Zapata is John Womack, Jr., *Zapata and the Mexican Revolution* (New York: Knopf, 1969).

5. Spota, "la Identidad," p. 23.

6. Freud says, "the fear of death should be regarded as analogous to the fear of castration." *Inhibitions, Symptoms and Anxiety, The Standard Edition of the Complete Psychological Works of Sigmund Freud*, ed. James Strachey, 24 vols. (London: Hogarth, 1959) 20:130.

7. *The Death Ship*, p. 118.

8. Newton Arvin interprets the motif of maiming in *Moby Dick* as representing fear of the father and his power to "impose constraint upon the most powerful instincts, both egoistic and sexual; the father also . . . threatens even to destroy the latter by castration and may indeed, in all but the literal sense, carry out the threat." *Herman Melville* (New York: Viking, 1957), p. 172.

9. The fear of castration represents, according to Freud, the fear of being unable to be reunited with the "mother . . . in the act of copulation." *Inhibitions, Symptoms and Anxiety*, p. 139.

10. *March to the Montería* (New York: Hill & Wang, 1971), p. 103.

11. *Government* (New York: Hill & Wang, 1971), p. 3. Subsequent page number references in this chapter are to this edition.

12. *The Cotton-Pickers* seems to indicate that Traven was influenced by the I.W.W. See William Weber Johnson, "*Cotton-Pickers* Sheds Light on Traven's Life," *Los Angeles Times Calendar*, 29 June 1969, p. 46; Charles Miller, "Our Great Neglected Wobbly," *Michigan Quarterly Review*, 6, no. 1 (1967): 59.

13. "Der Roman *Regierung*," *Die Buchergilde*, no. 9 (1931): 261.

14. Ibid.

15. *The Death Ship*, p. 187.

16. "Der Roman *Regierung*," p. 261.

17. Ibid.

18. For a classic novel of the Mexican Revolution of 1910, including an account of the tangled politics and a fascinating portrait of Pancho Villa, see Martín Luís Guzman, *The Eagle and the Serpent* (Garden City, N.Y.: Doubleday, Dolphin, 1965).

19. Recknagel, *Beiträge zur Biografie* (1971), p. 235.

20. Frans Blom and Gertrude Duby, *La Selva Lacandona* (Mexico, D. F.: Editorial Cultura, 1951), p. 110.

21. Manuel Pedro Gonzalez, *Trayectoria de la Novela en Mexico* (Mexico, D.F.: Ediciones Botas, 1951), p. 321.

22. Ibid., p. 317.

23. Ibid., pp. 317–18.

24. "El Misterio Literario," p. 9.

Notes to Chapter 6

1. A novel *Aslan Norval*, was published in 1960, ten years after "Macario."

2. "The Insulted and Injured," *The New York Review of Books*, 28 July 1966, p. 24.

3. "The Night Visitor," *The Night Visitor and Other Stories* (New York: Hill & Wang, 1966), p. 26. Pagination in the text is from this collection of stories.

4. The ashes of the Aztec prince foreshadow Traven's own cremation thirty years afterward, when it is his turn to go back to the earth of Chiapas province, the site of "The Night Visitor." Suarez, "Al Borde del Fin," p. 15.

5. "Conversations," p. 65.

6. *The Mother, Anxiety, and Death*, p. 34.

7. B. Traven, "Der Roman *Regierung*," p. 260.

8. According to Freud, Christianity revived the totem meal "in the form of communion, in which the company of brothers consumed the flesh and blood of the son—no longer the father—obtained sanctity thereby and identified themselves with him." *Totem and Taboo* (New York: Norton, 1950), p. 154.

9. Ibid.

10. Roger Pippett, reviewing *The Best American Short Stories of 1954*, ed. Martha Foley, singled out Traven's "The Third Guest" (the original title of "Macario") as the best in the volume. He said of the story: "It is a subtle variation on that oldest of literary forms, the fairy tale, and it is the best in the book." "New Hands and Old," *New York Times Book Review*, 22 August 1954, p. 5.

11. Recknagel also points out this source for "Macario" in his *Beiträge zur Biografie* (1971), p. 214.

12. "Godfather Death," *The Grimms' German Folk Tales*, trans. Francis P. Magoun, Jr. and Alexander H. Krapp (Carbondale: Southern Illinois University Press, 1960), p. 160.

13. *Inhibitions, Symptoms and Anxiety*, p. 140.

14. In the course of his interview with Judy Stone, Traven comments that for him "the pilgrim [Christ] represented the Church. And the Church is always asking for the last penny." "Conversations," p. 62.

15. *The Grimms' German Folk Tales*, p. 160.

16. *Moby-Dick*, p. 487.

Notes to Chapter 7

1. Traven is treated in two recent companion volumes edited by David Madden: *Tough Guy Writers of the Thirties*; and *Proletarian Writers of the Thirties* (Carbondale: Southern Illinois University Press, 1968).

2. "B(ashful) Traven," p. 2.

3. "Die Nationalität des B. Travens," *Die Buchergilde*, no. 9, 1931, p. 287.

4. Traven is referred to by Kingsley Widmer as one of the "more rugged or anarchistic defiers in the protest and proletarian literature." "The Way Out: Some Life-Style Sources of the Literary Tough Guy and the Proletarian Hero," *Tough Guy Writers*, p. 7. In *Proletarian Writers* there is an essay by Charles Miller, "B. Traven, Pure Proletarian Writer," but Miller himself seems to realize that the label "pure proletarian" is inappropriate, since he also calls Traven an "outsider, exile, philosophical revolutionist and benevolent anarchist," p. 114.

5. Charles Miller, "Neglected Wobbly," p. 59; "Introduction," B. Traven, *The Night Visitor and Other Stories*, p. xii. *The Cotton-Pickers* was originally published under the title "The Wobbly."

6. *The Cotton-Pickers* (New York: Hill & Wang, 1969), p. 200.

7. William Weber Johnson, "*Cotton-Pickers*," p. 46.

8. Mr. Hill, formerly Vice-President of Hill & Wang, supplied this information to me.

9. "la Identidad," p. 24.

10. "Neglected Wobbly," p. 59.

11. "Conversations," p. 59.

12. Loubet, "Falleció Ayer el Novelista B. Traven," p. 35.

13. *The Creation of the Sun and the Moon* (New York: Hill & Wang, 1968). This is substantially the same story that Estrellita tells Andrés in *The Carreta*.

14. By 1924 Hammett's tough-guy detective, the Continental Op, was fully developed in stories that appeared in the *Black Mask*. Chandler's original private eye appeared in this magazine in 1933. See Philip Durham, "The *Black Mask* School," *Tough Guy Writers*, pp. 51–79.

15. Sheldon Norman Grebstein, "The Tough Hemingway and His Hard-Boiled Children," *Tough Guy Writers*, p. 27.

16. *The General from the Jungle* (New York: Hill & Wang, 1973), pp. 249–50.

17. Neville Baybrooke compares *The Death Ship* with *The Iron Heel* in "The Hero Without a Name: Some Notes on Traven's *The Death Ship*," *Texas Quarterly* 6, no. 4 (1963): 143; Bernard Smith cites Jack London as the "literary antecedent" of Traven in "B(ashful) Traven," p. 2. One of the more bizarre theories of Traven's identity was that he was the "reincarnation of Jack London," "B. Traven, Secretive Author, is Dead," *New York Times*, 27 March 1969, p. 47.

18. Colcord, "A Powerful Book," p. 5.

19. "Sugi-Mugi," p. 131.

20. "The Insulted and Injured," *The New York Review of Books*, 28 July 1969, p. 24.

21. For all his obsession with death, Traven's life lasted at least seventy-nine years. According to his own claim he was born in 1890. Recknagel, however, reproduces a document in which "Ret Marut," registering with the Dusseldorf police in 1912, gave his birthdate as 25 February 1882. *Beiträge zur Biografie* (1971), p. 38. This would make Traven eighty-seven at the time of his death.

22. p. 279.

23. "la Identidad," p. 21.

24. *The Death Ship*, p. 48.

25. R. D. Laing, *The Divided Self* (New York, 1960), p. 149.

26. Suarez, "El Misterio Literario," p. 4.

27. Hans Erich Lampl, "Stevnemøte Med Traven," *Aftenposten*, 15 April, 1969, p. 1.

28. Ibid., p. 14.

29. Johnson, "B. Traven: His Secrets," p. 9.

30. Ibid.

31. Suarez, "El Misterio Literario," p. 9.

32. Mary Blume, "Clearing Up the Mysteries," p. 21.

33. p. 111.

34. Loubet, "Falleció Ayer el Novelista, B. Traven," p. 35.

35. p. 287.

36. Laing, *The Divided Self*, p. 149.

37. (New York: Bantam, 1967), p. 33, 34.

38. *The Divided Self*, p. 125.

39. Ibid., p. 126.

40. "Al Borde Del Fin," p. 14.

41. *The Death Ship*, p. 232.

42. Isse Nunez, "Murió B. Traven, el Celebre Escritor Cuva Identidad Estaba en el Misterio," *Novedades*, 27 March 1959, p. 6.

Works
Consulted

Aaron, Daniel. *Writers on the Left.* New York: Avon Books, 1965.

"Adventure, Unglossed." *Time,* 17 June 1935, p. 74.

"Also Out this Week Fiction." *New Yorker,* 28 April 1934, p. 102.

Arvin, Newton. *Herman Melville.* New York: Viking, 1957.

Baumann, Michael Leopold. "A Discussion of Four B. Traven Questions With Particular Attention to *The Death Ship.*" Ph.D. Dissertation, University of Pennsylvania, 1971.

Baybrooke, Neville. "The Hero Without a Name: Some Notes on Traven's *The Death Ship.*" *Texas Quarterly* 6, no. 4 (1963): 140–44.

Blom, Frans, and Duby, Gertrude. *La Selva Lacandona.* Mexico, D. F.: Editorial Cultura, 1955.

Blume, Mary. "Clearing up the Mysteries of Author B. Traven." *Los Angeles Times,* 19 July 1970, p. 1.

Bonaparte, Marie. *The Life and Works of Edgar Allen Poe: A Psychoanalytic Interpretation.* London: Imago Publishing Co., 1949.

Bourget-Pailleron, Robert. "Souvenirs et Romans." *Revue des Deux Mondes* 45 (May 1938): 223–24.

Le Boutellier, Peggy. "Who is B. Traven? What is He?" *Modern Mexico,* January 1948, pp. 14–15.

"Briefly Noted Fiction." *New Yorker,* 10 May 1952, pp. 137–38.

"B. Traven Betrayed." *Life:* "Letters to the Editors," 15 March 1948, p. 23.

"The B. Traven Mystery." *Time:* "Letters," 15 March 1948, pp. 12, 14.

"B. Traven, Secretive Author is Dead." *New York Times,* 27 March 1969, p. 47.

"B. Traven, Writer of Powerful Tales Who Hid His Identity." *The Times* (London), 28 March 1969, p. 12.

Buchan, Willard. "Fantasy, perhaps." *Spectator*, 7 July 1967, pp. 23–24.

Calder-Marshall, Arthur. "The Novels of B. Traven." *Horizon*, July 1940, pp. 523–26.

"Candido and the Capitalists." *Time*, 21 April 1952, p. 14.

"Central American Anecdote." *Time*, 18 July 1939, pp. 50–51.

Cerruto, Oscar. "Bruno Traven, El Escrito Incognito." Introduction to *El Barco de Los Muertes*, pp. 7–14, Mexico [no publ.], 1945.

Chamberlain, John. *New York Times*, 18 May 1934, p. 21.

————. *New York Times*, 11 June 1935, p. 19.

Cheuse, Alan. Review of *"General from the Jungle."* New York Times Book Review, 26 August 1973, p. 24.

"A Choice of Good Entertainments." *Times Literary Supplement*, 16 March 1940, p. vii.

Colcord, Lincoln. "A Powerful Book Unfettered, Wild." *The New York Herald Tribune Books*, 13 May 1934, p. 5.

Connolly, Cyril. "New Novels." *The New Statesman—Nation*, 27 April 1935, p. 594.

Conrad, Joseph. "The Brute." *A Set of Six*. Garden City, N.Y.: Doubleday, 1924.

Conroy, Jack. "In the Spirit of the Wobblies." *Chicago Daily News*, 29 April 1969, p. 9.

Dante. *The Inferno*, translated by John Ciardi. New York: New American Library, Mentor, 1954.

"Diskussion um 'Macario.'" *B-T Mitteilungen*, October 1952, p. 63.

Doerflinger, Larry. "Hell Afloat." *The Saturday Review of Literature*, 5 May 1934, p. 677.

"Er ist ein Sohn des Kaisers," *Stern*, 13 April 1969, pp. 184, 186.

Etheridge, James M.; Kopala, Barbara; and Riley, Carolyn. "B. Traven." *Contemporary Authors*. Detroit: Gale Research Co., 1968, pp. 433–35.

Fadiman, Clifton. "The Great Traven Mystery." *The New Yorker*, 15 June 1935, pp. 85–86.

Feeney, Willard. "Ripeness is All: Late Late Romanticism and Other Recent Fiction." *The Southern Review*, n.s. 3, no. 4 (1967): 1050–61.

Ferguson, Otis. "Action Stuff." *The New Republic*, 27 July 1938, p. 341.

"Fiction." *Times Literary Supplement*, 15 February 1934, p. 109.

Works Consulted

"Fiction." *Times Literary Supplement*, 11 October 1934, p. 697.

Flandrau, Grace. "A Drama of Simple People." *The Saturday Review of Literature*, 30 July 1938, p. 6.

Foote, Peter G., and Wilson, David M. *The Viking Achievement*. New York: Praeger, 1970.

Fraser, John. "Rereading Traven's *The Death Ship*." *Southern Review* 9, no. 1 (January 1973): 69–92.

———. "Splendour in the Darkness: B. Traven's *The Death Ship*." *Dalhousie Review* 44 (1964): 34–43.

Freud, Sigmund. *Beyond the Pleasure Principle*. New York: Bantam, 1967.

———. *Collected Papers*, vol. 4. New York: Basic Books, 1959.

———. *Inhibitions, Symptoms and Anxiety, The Standard Edition of the Complete Psychological Works of Sigmund Freud*, edited by James Strachey, vol. 20. London: Hogarth Press, 1959.

———. *Jokes and their Relation to the Unconscious*. New York: Norton, 1963.

———. "Psychoanalytic Notes Upon an Autobiographical Account of a Case of Paranoia (Dementia Paranoides) (1911)." *Three Case Histories*. New York: Collier, 1963.

———. *Totem and Taboo*. New York: Norton, 1950.

Frohock, W.M. *The Novel of Violence in America*. Boston: Beacon, 1964.

Gale, Gerard. (Max Schmid). Introduction, Epilogue, to *Khundar*. Egnach, Switzerland: Clou Verlag, 1963, pp. i–iii, 73–103.

Geismer, Maxwell. "Peons in Agony." *The Saturday Review*, 19 April 1952, pp. 15–16.

George, Manfred. "B. Traven's Identity." *New Republic*, 24 March 1947, p. 35.

Gonzalez, Manuel Pedro. "Bruno Traven, auténtico novelista mexicano." *Trayectoria de la Novela en Mexico*. Mexico, D.F.: Ediciones Botas, 1951, pp. 316–21.

Grafs, Oskar Maria. "Wer war Traven?" *Aufbau*, 11 April 1969, p. 28.

Greene, Marjorie. "B. Traven in Love with a Latin Dilemma." *Los Angeles Times Calendar*, 9 April 1967.

Gregory, Horace. "In the Mexican Mountains." *The New York Herald Tribune Books*, 9 June 1935, p. 5.

Grimm, Jacob. *Teutonic Mythology*. Vol. 4. New York: Dover, 1966.

Grimm, Jacob, and Grimm, Wilhelm. "Godfather Death." *The Grimms' German Folk Tales*, translated by Francis P. Magoun, Jr. and Alexander H. Krappe. Carbondale: Southern Illinois University Press, 1960.

Works Consulted

Guzman, Martín Luis. *The Eagle and the Serpent*. Garden City: Doubleday, Dolphin, 1965.

"Habla Luis Spota; El Indisputable Descubridor (de B. Traven)." *Mañana*, 19 April 1969, pp. 50–53.

"Hace 21 Años, *Mañana* Descrifo El Enigma B. Traven." *Mañana*, 5 April 1969, p. 46–53.

Hagemann, E.R. "A Checklist of the Work of B. Traven and the Critical Estimates and Biographical Essays on Him; together with a Brief Biography." *Papers of the Bibliographical Society of America* 53 (First Quarter, 1959): 37–67.

———. "Huye! A Conjectural Biography of B. Traven." *Revista InterAmericana de Bibliografia* 10 (1960): 370–86.

Hanley, James. "Sugi-Mugi." *The Spectator*, 26 January 1934, p. 131.

Hart, James D. "B. Traven." *The Oxford Companion to American Literature*. New York: Oxford University Press, 1965.

Hays, H.R. "The Importance of B. Traven." *Chimera* 4, no. 4 (1946): 44–54.

Heidemann, Gerd. "Das Rätsel Traven gelöst," *Stern*, 25 August 1963, pp. 8–11.

———. "Wer ist der Mann, der Traven Heisst?" *Stern*, 7 May 1967, pp. 58–71, 170–73.

Heller, Arthur. "A Great Unknown." *New Masses*, 12 June 1934, p. 24.

Herndon, James. "How to Survive in the Jungle." *New York Times Book Review*, 31 October 1971, pp. 52–53.

Hibbs, Kerry. "Traven Always Favored Underdog, Widow Says." *The Arizona Daily Star*, 21 April 1974, p. 6.

Hicks, Granville. *The Great Tradition*. New York: Macmillan, 1935.

———. "Proletarian Mystery." *New Masses*, 16 July 1935, p. 2.

———. "Romancers of the Left." *New Masses*, 23 August 1938, pp. 22–23.

Hill, Lawrence. "Letters: B(ashful) Traven." *New York Times Book Review*, 27 December 1970, p. 10.

Humphrey, Charles Robert. "B. Traven: An Examination of the Controversy Over His Identity with an Analysis of His Major Work and His Place in Literature." Ph.D. dissertation, University of Texas, 1965.

Hunter, Clyde. "Winner Lose All." *The New Republic*, 31 July 1935, p. 342.

Irsfeld, John Henry. "The American as a Symbol of the Conflict Between Industry and Nature in the First Five Novels of B. Traven." Ph.D. Dissertation, University of Texas, 1969.

Works Consulted

Jannach, Hubert. "B. Traven—an American or German Author." *German Quarterly* 35, no. 4 (November 1963): 459–68.

———. "B. Traven." *Aslan Norval, Books Abroad* 35, no. 1 (Winter 1961): 59.

———. "The B. Traven Mystery." *Books Abroad* 35, no. 1 (Winter 1961): 28–29.

Johnson, William [Weber]. "B. Traven." *New York Times*, letter to the editor, 4 May 1969, p. 44.

———. "B. Traven: A Literary Lode Who Prefers Anonymity." *Los Angeles Times Calendar*, 8 October 1967, p. 1.

———. "B. Traven: His Secrets and Passion for Anonymity." *Book Week*, 25 May 1969, p. 9.

———. "The Carreta." *New York Times Book Review*, 29 March 1970, p. 5.

———. "The Traven Case." *New York Times Book Review*, 17 April 1966, p. 1.

———. "Who is Bruno Traven." *Life*, 10 March 1947, pp. 13–14.

Kazin, Alfred. "*The Bridge in the Jungle* and Other Works of Fiction." *New York Times Book Review*, 24 July 1938, p. 6.

Kelleghan, Kevin M. "Mrs. Traven Lifts the Veil of Secrecy." *New York Post*, 3 April 1969, p. 40.

Kirby, T. A. "The Pardoner's Tale and the Treasure of the Sierra Madre." *Modern Language Notes* 66 (1951): 269–70.

Krim, Seymour. "The Passion of the Peons." *The Commonweal*, 13 June 1952, pp. 15–16.

Kunitz, Stanley J., and Haycraft, Howard, eds. "B. Traven." In *Twentieth Century Authors, A Biographical Dictionary of Modern Literature*. New York: H.W. Wilson and Co., 1942, pp. 1417–18.

———. "B. Traven." In *Twentieth Century Authors: First Supplement*. New York: H.W. Wilson and Co., 1955, p. 1005.

Laing, R.D. *The Divided Self*. New York: Pantheon, 1969.

Lampl, Hans Erich. "Stevnemøte Med Traven." *Aftenposten*, 15 April 1969, pp. 1–3, 14.

Lawrence, D.H. *Studies in Classic American Literature*. Garden City, N.Y.: Doubleday, 1951.

"Leserbriefe Abschied von B. Traven." *Aufbau*, 13 June 1969, p. 8.

"Limited View." *Times Literary Supplement*, 8 February 1952, p. 105.

"Lo Que Pasa en Mexico." *Nuevo Mundo*, November 1969, pp. 90–91.

Loubet, Enrique, Jr. "Falleció Ayer el Novelista, B. Traven." *Excelsior*, 27 March 1969, pp. 1, 5, 35.

Works Consulted

Lynn, D. "The Works of B. Traven." *Arena* 1 (1950): 89–94.

McAlpine, William Reid. "B. Traven: The Man and His Work." *Tomorrow*, August 1948, pp. 43–46.

McHenry, J. Patrick. *A Short History of Mexico.* New York: Doubleday, 1962.

MacDougall, Robert B. "An Ironic Story of the Greed for Gold." *The Saturday Review of Literature*, 22 June 1935, p. 14.

MacNamara, Desmond. "Mystery Man." *New Statesman*, 23 June 1967, p. 880.

Madden, David, ed. *Tough Guy Writers of the Thirties.* Carbondale: Southern Illinois University Press, 1968.

Mair, John. "New Novels." *The New Statesman and Nation*, 9 March 1940, pp. 338, 340.

Mano, D.K. Review of *"The Rebellion of the Hanged." New York Times Book Review*, 7 August 1972, p. 2.

Marsh, Fred T. "The Treasure of the Sierra Madre and Other Works of Fiction." *New York Times Book Review*, 9 June 1935, p. 6.

[Marut, Ret.] *Khundar.* Egnach, Switzerland: Clou Verlag, n.d., 1963.

Melville, Herman. *Billy Budd, Sailor*, edited by Harrison Hayford and Merton M. Sealts, Jr. Chicago: University of Chicago Press, Phoenix Books, 1962.

———. *Moby Dick.* New York: Hendricks House, 1962.

Miller, Charles. "B. Traven, Continued." *New York Times Book Review*, 20 November 1966, p. 84.

———. "B. Traven, Pure Proletarian Writer." *Proletarian Writers of the Thirties*, ed. David Madden. Carbondale: Southern Illinois University Press, 1968.

———. "Introduction to B. Traven." *The Night Visitor and Other Stories.* New York: Hill & Wang, 1966, pp. vii–xii.

———. "Our Great Neglected Wobbly." *Michigan Quarterly Review* 6, no. 1 (1967): 57–61.

———, and Lujan, R. E., eds. "B. Traven, A Special Section." *Texas Quarterly* 6, no. 4, (1963): 161–211.

"Mystery Man." *Newsweek*, 21 April 1952, p. 124.

"Die Nationalität des B. Travens." *Die Buchergilde*, no. 9 (1931): 287.

Neikanen, E., Jr. "Letter Disputes Review by D. K. Mano of *The Rebellion of the Hanged." New York Times Book Review*, 17 September 1972, p. 51.

Neuhauser, Peter. "Der Mann, der sich B. Traven nennt." *Die Zeit*, 16 May 1967, p. 10.

Neville, Helen. "The Noble Savage." *The Nation*, 6 August 1938, pp. 133–34.

Works Consulted

"New Picture: The Treasure of the Sierra Madre." *Time*, 2 February 1948, pp. 5, 80, 82.

Nichols, Lewis. "American Notebook, B. Traven Again." *New York Times Book Review*, 11 June 1967, p. 51.

"Nota." B. Traven, *Puente en la Selva*. Mexico, D. F.: A. P. Marquez, 1941, pp. 5–8.

Nunez, Isse. 'Murió B. Traven, el Celebre Escritor Cuva Identitad Estaba en el Misterio." *Novedades*, 27 March 1959, pp. 1, 6.

"On the Trail of B. Traven." *The Publisher's Weekly*, 9 July 1938, pp. 105–6.

"Other New Books Fiction." *Times Literary Supplement*, 2 May 1935, p. 289.

"Other New Books Fiction." *Times Literary Supplement*, 30 November 1935, p. 817.

Parkes, Henry Bamford. *A History of Mexico*. Boston: Houghton Mifflin, 1966.

Parmenter, Ross. "*The Creation of the Sun and the Moon*, by B. Traven." *New York Times Book Review*, 2 February 1969, p. 36.

Pippett, Roger. "New Hands and Old." *New York Times Book Review*, 22 August 1954, p. 5.

Plomer, William. "Fiction." *The Spectator*, 28 September 1934, 454.

Powell, Lawrence Clark. "Who is B. Traven?" *New Masses*, 2 August 1938, pp. 22–23.

Pritchett, V. S. "The Fortnightly Library." *The Fortnightly Review*, n.s. 136, November 1934, p. 639.

———. "New Novels." *The New Statesman and Nation*, 8 September 1934, p. 296.

Quercus, P. E. G. "Trade Winds." *Saturday Review of Literature*, 28 April 1934, p. 671.

Raskin, Jonah. "B. Traven: Writer from the Jungle." *University Review* 31 (October 1973): 17, 19.

Recknagel, Rolf. *B. Traven: Beiträge zur Biografie*. Leipzig: Reclam, [1966].

———. *B. Traven: Beiträge zur Biografie*. Leipzig: Reclam, 1971.

———. "B. Traven und Ret Marut, Eine Literaturkritische Untersuchung von Rolf Recknagel." *Die Kultur*, 8 December 1959, pp. 4–5.

Rexroth, Kenneth. "Disengagement: The Art of the Beat Generation." *The Alternative Society Essays from the Other World*. New York: Herder and Herder, 1970.

Rheingold, Joseph C. *The Mother, Anxiety, and Death: The Catastrophic Death Complex*. Boston: Little, Brown & Co., 1967.

Works Consulted

Rideout, Walter B. *The Radical Novel in the United States 1900–1954*. Cambridge: Harvard University Press, 1956.

Rivas, Pedro Geoffrey. Introduction to Bruno Traven, *La Rebelion de los Colgados*. Mexico, D. F.: Ediciones Insignia, 1938, pp. 5–9.

S.W. "Mexican Adventure." *Manchester Guardian Weekly*, 5 October 1934, p. 275.

Schwartz, Harry. *This Book Collecting Racket*. Chicago: Normandie House, 1937.

"A Seaman's Story." *New York Times*, 29 April 1934, p. 21.

"The Secret of El Gringo." *Time*, 16 August 1948, pp. 34, 36.

Shabecoff, Philip. "B. Traven Called Son of the Kaiser." *New York Times*, 7 May 1967, p. 59.

Sheppard, Richard F. Review of *"The Bridge in the Jungle."* *New York Times*, 24 April 1967, p. 31.

Smith, Bernard. "B(ashful) Traven." *New York Times Book Review*, 22 November 1970, p. 1.

Soskin, William. "Mysterious B. Traven." *The New York Herald Tribune Books*, 14 August 1938, p. 5.

Spitzegger, Leopold. "Wer Ist B. Traven." *Plan* 1 (August 1946): 688–71.

Spota, Luis. *"Mañana* Descubre la Identidad de B. Traven." *Mañana*, 7 August 1948, pp. 10–26.

Stone, Judy. "Conversations with B. Traven." *Ramparts*, October 1967, pp. 55–75.

———. "The Mystery of B. Traven." *Ramparts*, September 1967, pp. 31–49.

———. "Revolution: When There's Nothing to Lose." *Los Angeles Times Calendar*, 20 May 1973, pp. 1–3.

Strasser, Dr. Charlot. *4 Neue Amerikanische Dichter: Jack London, Upton Sinclair, Sinclair Lewis, B. Traven. 7 Vorlesungen.* Zurich: Schweizer Verband des Personals öffentliche Dienste, 1929.

"Stumbling." *Times Literary Supplement*, 5 June 1969, p. 601.

Suarez, Luis. "Al Borde del Fin, Traven Pensó En un Escopetazo al Estilo Hemingway." *Siempre!*, 9 April 1969, pp. 12–15.

———. *"Siempre!* Desentraña, al Fin, La Misteriosa Actividad de Traven en La Selva de Chiapas." *Siempre!*, 7 May 1969, pp. 34–36, 70.

———. *"Siempre!* Revela, al Fin, El Misterio Literario Mas Apasionante Del Siglo y Presenta al Mundo a B. Traven!" *Siempre!*, 19 October 1966, pp. 4–9, 70.

Sylvester, Harry. "The Snapping of Chains." *The New York Times Book Review*, 20 April 1952, p. 4.

Thompson, Ralph. *The New York Times*, 18 July 1938, p. 11.

Traven, B. "Amerika, das Gelobte Land der Freiheit," *Die Buchergilde*, no. 1 (1930): 12–14.

———. *Aslan Norval*. Vienna: Kurt Desch, 1960.

———. *The Bridge in the Jungle*. New York: Hill & Wang, 1966.

———. *The Carreta*. New York: Hill & Wang, 1970.

———. *The Cotton Pickers*. New York: Hill & Wang, 1969.

———. *The Creation of the Sun and the Moon*. New York: Hill & Wang, 1969.

———. *The Death Ship, The Story of an American Sailor*. New York: Collier, 1962.

———. *The General from the Jungle*. London: Robert Hale. 1954.

———. *Government*. New York: Hill & Wang, 1971.

———. *Land Des Fruhlings*. Zurich: Buchergilde Gutenberg, 1950.

———. "A Letter to Harry W. Schwartz and a Letter to Dr. F. J. Raddatz." *Texas Quarterly*, no. 4 (1963): 206–7.

———. Letter to Manfred George, 1929, quoted by Professor Rolf Recknagel in a letter to me.

———. *March to the Montería*. New York: Hill & Wang, 1971.

———. "Mein Roman: *Das Totenschiff*." *Die Buchergilde*, no. 3 (1926): 34–38.

———. *The Night Visitor and other Stories*. New York: Hill & Wang, 1966.

———. *The Rebellion of the Hanged*. New York: Knopf, 1952.

———. "Der Roman *Regierung*." *Die Buchergilde*, no. 9 (1931): 260–61.

———. *La Rosa Blanca*. Mexico, D. F.: Compania General De Ediciones, 1951.

———. *Stories by the Man Nobody Knows: Nine Tales by B. Traven*. Evanston, Illinois: Regency Books, 1961.

———. "Traven über sein Buch 'Die Brücke im Dschungel.' " *Die Buchergilde*, no. 3 (1929): 35–37, quoted by Professor Rolf Recknagel in a letter to me.

———. *The Treasure of the Sierra Madre*. New York: Hill & Wang, 1968.

———. *Trozas*. Munich: Wilhelm Heyne, 1959.

Troy, William. "Radix Malorum." *The Nation*, 17 July 1935, p. 79.

"Uncivilization." *Times Literary Supplement*, 2 March 1940, p. 109.

Usigli, Rudolfo and Suarez, Luis. "Traven: Al Morir El Hombre Invisible Recobra Su Cuerpo." *Siempre!*, 22 May 1969, pp. i–viii.

Works Consulted

Van Doren, Mark. "Men Without Countries." *The Nation*, 16 May 1934, pp. 569–70.

Wain, John. "The Insulted and Injured." *The New York Review of Books*, 28 July 1966, pp. 22–24.

West, Anthony. "The Great Traven Mystery." *New Yorker*, 22 July 1967, pp. 82–87.

Whitman, Alden. "6 Traven Novels to be Published Here." *New York Times*, 5 December 1971, p. 86.

Whitney, Dwight. "More About Traven." *Life*, 2 February 1948, p. 66.

"Who is Traven?" "Letters to the Editors," *Life*, 31 March 1947, p. 9.

"Who is Traven?" *Times Literary Supplement*, 22 June 1967, p. 553.

Wieder, Josef. "B. Traven und Ret Marut." *Die Kultur*, February 1960, p. 17.

Womack, John, Jr. *Zapata and the Mexican Revolution.* New York: Knopf, 1969.